A GUIDE

TO

PLANNING A WEDDING

THE EASYWAY
ANNA BENNETT

Editor: Roger Sproston

Easyway Guides

ISBN

978-1-80236-125-4

Printed by 4edge www.4edge.co.uk

Cover design by BW Studio Derby

Contents

Introduction

Useful addresses

Best websites for wedding planners

Appendix 1-sample wedding speeches

Index

****

Introduction

Getting married must surely rank as one of the biggest events in a person's life. This is a day that will never be forgotten, and this book will try to ensure that it will never be forgotten for all the right reasons. Planning is the key to a successful wedding, wherever it takes place and the information contained within will help you to plan effectively.

I have made reference, at the end of the introduction, to the government regulations which affect marriage ceremonies and receptions, mainly that the number of people able to attend a marriage is now unlimited.

Conventional heterosexual weddings form the main subject matter of the book although of course it is also totally relevant to civil partnerships and same-sex marriages. Those who have entered a civil partnership or same-sex marriage can also utilise the many useful areas of this book, such as planning and budgeting for a wedding. The first chapter covers general points relating to marriage, such as the law and other areas such as tax and property. Although not as 'sexy' as the actual wedding day, the basic law that underpins marriage is of the utmost importance.

The intention is to provide an overview of the institution of marriage and ensure that those who are participating in the big day have a sound understanding of the institution of marriage and the subsequent commitment that this entails. The subsequent chapters cover all the elements of a wedding, such as the initial engagement and the planning of the big day, including the main players such as the best man and bridesmaids, not forgetting the bride and groom! The biggest expense of the wedding day is covered, the reception, which always needs careful planning. Also Included are outline budgeting frameworks to ensure that all costs are covered.

Alternative wedding ceremonies (other than traditional Church of England) are also covered, such as Buddhist, Muslim Pagan, Unitarian, Christian Scientist and Non-Conformist.

Getting married is a big event for all concerned, not least the bride and groom or civil partners. If it goes well, it will be a day to remember. It may be expensive but it is so important that accurate planning is needed. Of course, there are those who do not desire a big wedding and this book will also show you how to do it on a shoestring. Whichever way you choose to go this book should help immeasurably in the planning of the big day.

With all weddings and civil partnerships becoming ever more expensive (the average cost now being £21,000 in 2022, although this can stretch to £40,000 depending on what is required and how deep the pockets of the bride and groom are see below insurance) advice and guidance on how to plan and budget for a wedding is now more needed than ever. It is a fact that not many couples go for the cheaper option, i.e., registrar and a booze up later. Research has revealed that a quarter of married couples/civil partners in 2022 went into debt to enable them to meet the escalating costs. One in ten couples finished with debts of more than £10,000.

There are useful hints throughout the book on how to minimise costs. One thing is very apparent and that is that venues that hire out halls tend to charge anything up to 60% more for wedding/civil partnership packages than they do for normal hire. The costs of meals and drinks also goes up. One tip is don't be afraid to haggle, a 10% reduction can help. Also make sure you get all contracts in writing. You can also haggle with photographers who typically push up their prices for weddings. If you have a friend who is handy with a camera this is one way to save money. Also, see below for wedding insurance!

Once you know how much you are prepared to spend work out how much you need to save and in what time frame. Make sure that you have a strict budget and that you stick to it. Choose the day that you want to get married. Even better, choose the month. A Friday wedding can cut the cost of the venue by 20%. A winter wedding is also a good deal cheaper, although avoid December. June and September are the most popular and expensive months.

If you are booking your honeymoon, February is the cheapest time as you can get bargains on flights and accommodation before March price rises.

Cash gifts are increasingly expected instead of actual physical gifts. This is a good way for parents and grandparents to avoid inheritance tax too (IHT) All or part of a cash gift will be exempt from IHT, provided that it is made on or shortly after the wedding or civil partnership wedding date. Each parent, including stepparents, can give up to £5,000 tax-free and grandparents can give up to £2,500. Any other person, relative or friend can give up to £1,000. it is worth couples who each own property thinking about capital gains tax (CGT) implications once they are married. Best to try to sort out the sale of one or another of the properties before you move in together.

Wedding Insurance

Given the high costs of weddings and the risk involved in the organisation, it is recommended that you take out a form of wedding insurance. According to Hitched a wedding planning site www.hitched.co.uk the average spent on the big day last year (2021) was £32,273 that represents a big increase over the previous year. This sum includes such things as venue hire, food, videos, dress and other outfits and the honeymoon. A wedding planning app, Bridebook, puts the figure at a more modest £24,000.

Whatever the sum, with such high outlays at stake most couples feel better if they have some sort of guarantee that all will go well which is why many people buy a form of wedding insurance to protect themselves. However, if you do go down this road make sure that you read the small print and that all elements of the wedding, including the venue are covered. Not all insurance policies do, and this could leave you out of pocket.

Here are a few tips:

- Don't be underinsured. Wedding budgets tend to creep up, so even after you have bought a policy, check that you have enough cover and ask your insurer to extend it if necessary. There are a whole range of policies. For example, John Lewis provides £100,000 of cover for £310. Insurers have different cover limits for items such as cancellation, clothing, photography, and gifts. If you are spending a disproportionate amount on a single item then make sure you are fully covered for that item. Dreamsaver's wedding insurance, for example, provides different levels of cover www.weddinginsurance.co.uk.
- Liability cover. Many venues require the bride and groom to have their own liability cover in case of accident or damage to the property. Again, this is something that an insurance company such as dreamsaver can advise on.
- Save money on cashback sites. You can save between £10.50 and £21 when buying John Lewis wedding insurance through top cashback and £25.50 on a Debenhams policy or £26.25 on Dreamsaver premiums.

No wedding insurance covers 'cold feet' and they won't cover your honeymoon. You will need separate travel insurance for that.

Scams

One in ten couples have fallen victim to wedding-related scams according to Barclays. It is warning anyone planning a wedding to check suppliers carefully before booking or handing over deposits. Research by the bank found that 20 per cent of wedding scams involved phantom photographers, 16 per cent florists and 16 per cent non-existent wedding planners.

Couples should read online reviews and ask for references and written confirmation of any agreements made. Check for the 'padlock' symbol on web addresses that signifies security before handing over payments. The following areas are ripe for scammers:

- *Venues that shut down* –having taken your deposit, or the deposits of many people, certain unscrupulous vendors make off with people's money.

- *Unreliable or overpriced vendors*-when it comes to photographers, florists, bands, or DJs, figuring out the costs and reliability can be confusing. That's why it's so important to do as much research and vetting as you can before you make a deal.

- *Buying your wedding gown online*-the thought of spending thousands on a wedding dress may fill you with dread, but sometimes you get what you pay for if you choose to purchase your dress online. If possible, don't buy your wedding dress online because the risks are very high for getting a completely different dress than what you ordered, In many cases, you won't be able to return it if there are no terms and conditions on the site.

- *Paying in cash*-a weddings can be a massive expense. While there are many ways to cut costs, paying for goods and services in cash is a major red flag. You should pay for everything with a credit card if you can,

COVID 19: From 19 July 2021 the rules for wedding and civil partnership ceremonies; and wedding receptions and civil partnership celebrations changed:

- There are no legal restrictions on the number of people that can attend a wedding, civil partnership, reception, or celebration.
- Legal requirements for social distancing no longer apply and you do not need to stay 2 metres apart from people you do not live with.
- Face coverings are no longer required by law in any setting. However, the government expects and recommends that people wear face coverings in crowded areas such as public transport.
- If someone has been instructed by NHS Test and Trace to self-isolate they must still self-isolate and not attend.

****

MARRIAGE AND COHABITATION

Chapter 1

Marriage and Cohabitation – The Law and Conventions

Before we discuss the preparations for getting married, which is the main aim of this book, we should look at the institution of marriage and how it works within the law. We will look at who can get married, the Engagement, marriage formalities, effects of marriage, cohabitation and agreements. Having a background knowledge of the law concerning marriage will help raise awareness of the whole area surrounding marriage and civil partnerships.

The law of England stated that marriage is the 'voluntary union for life of one man and one woman to the exclusion of all others. However, with the introduction of civil partnerships and the Marriage (Same Sex Couples) Act 2013 this now also applies to same sex couples.

Much has changed in family life over the years and today, marriages break up with alarming frequency and more and more people choose to live together as opposed to marrying.

Marriage

The law states that, in order to marry, a person must:

a) be unmarried

b) be over the age of 18

You are also legally a single person if your previous marriage has been annulled. Basically, anyone who wants to marry must be a single person in the eyes of the law. A person must be over 18. If a person is aged between 16-18 parental consent must be gained. A marriage where one of the persons is under 16 is absolutely void. If someone marries between the ages of 16-18 the marriage is voidable as opposed to void (see below). Parents, guardians, or the courts must consent to a marriage for someone between 16-18 years old.

No marriage can take place between close relations, i.e. blood relations, or non-blood relations where the relation is so close that a ban on Intermarriage is still imposed. Adopted children are generally treated in law as blood relatives. Brothers-in-law and sisters-in-law can marry as can step-parent and stepchild if the stepchild has not been raised as a child of the family and is over 21 years old.

Marriages must be voluntary

A marriage must be voluntary and not brought about through coercion. This brings about a problem in law when arranged marriages take place, as is the custom in certain ethnic groups. In general, the law does not interfere with arranged marriages. However, the courts will get involved if it is felt that there is duress and there is a threat of injury to life or liberty or a child is threatened with expulsion from home or community.

Marriages which can be annulled

Void marriages

Certain marriages are regarded in law as void. This means that, in the eyes of the law the marriage has never taken place at all. Marriages are void where:

- one of the parties is under 18
- the parties are closely related
- one of the parties is not a single person, i.e. the marriage is bigamous or polygamous.
- The parties are regarded in law as being of the same sex.

Certain marriages are regarded in law as valid until they are annulled. These are 'voidable' marriages and, in the eyes of the law can be annulled by either party.

Grounds for annulment

For a court to annul a voidable marriage the following grounds have to be demonstrated:

a) the marriage has not been consummated

21

b) the husband or wife had not understood the nature of the ceremony

c) the marriage was to someone of unsound mind

d) the marriage was to someone with venereal disease.

Getting engaged to be married

An engagement is not a precondition of marriage, as it once was. This is often the case, however. A couple will, after engagement, publicly announce their intention to be married. Legal disputes can, however, arise and couples can dispute ownership of property and gifts. An engagement ring is regarded as an outright gift in the eyes of the law.

If money has been expended on larger items, such as a house, in the anticipation of marriage, and the marriage has fallen through then this will become a legal dispute with each case turning on its own merit and the circumstances of any contract, written or unwritten. Certain insurance companies can offer insurance against weddings falling through or being cancelled. Cover can also be obtained for honeymoons falling through.

If a couple's wedding falls through they are legally obliged to return any wedding gifts received to their senders.

Marriage formalities

For a marriage to be valid, a formal licence and a formal ceremony are necessary. Authority to licence marriages is given to a priest of the Anglican Church and to civil officials (registrars). Every couple, therefore, must obtain permission to marry from an Anglican church or from a civil official. Many couples, because of cost, choose to marry in a registry office.

Religious ceremonies

Religious ceremonies are categorized according to whether they are solemnized by:

- The Anglican Church, including the Church of Wales
- Jews or Quakers (for whom special rules apply under the Marriage Act 1949)
- Some other recognized religion.

We have lived in a diverse ethnic society for many years and the rules governing marriage and religion are largely outmoded and in need of change. This will inevitably happen over time.

Church of England-licence to marry

About half of all religious marriage ceremonies take place in the Church of England. There are four ways to effect the necessary preliminaries for an Anglican marriage. Only one may be used.

To obtain consent to marry in the Church of England you must either:

- publish banns

or obtain one of the following:

- a common ecclesiastical licence
- a 'special licence' also from the Ecclesiastical authorities
- a superintendent registrars' certificate from the civil authorities.

Publishing banns

The banns, or the names of the couple who intend to marry, must be read aloud (published) in the church of the parish where the couple are resident. If the couple are resident in different parishes, then the banns must be read in each parish church, in one or other of which the ceremony will take place. The priest needs seven days notice in writing from both parties before the banns can be read. The priest must read them audibly in church on three successive Sundays. If there is no objection from any member of the congregation then, after the third reading the marriage can take place. If any objections are raised and voiced audibly by a member of the congregation then the banns are void.

Common licence

This dispenses with the banns and is given by the bishop of the diocese. You must make an affidavit that there is no impediment to the marriage and that any necessary parental consent has been given and that you have resided in the parish for 15 days.

Once granted, the licence to marry has immediate effect and is valid for three months. It will specify the church or chapel in which the marriage is to take place.

Special licence

This is issued by the Archbishop of Canterbury and enables a marriage to take place at any time or place. It also dispenses with the 15-day residence period. To get such a licence, which would for example be applicable if one of the parties was seriously ill, a sworn statement is required.

Superintendent registrars' certificate

Although it is the norm for a marriage in the Church of England to take place after banns have been read, or after obtaining a licence from church authorities, an Anglican wedding can take place after a superintendent registrars' certificate has been obtained. The parties must give notice to a superintendent registrar in the district in which they have resided for at least seven days before giving notice. They must make a solemn declaration that there are no lawful impediments to their union and that they meet the residential requirements. In the case of persons between 16-18, that they have parental consent. If the parties live in different districts, then notice must be given in each district. The notice is displayed in the superintendent's office for 21 days. At the end of that period, provided there are no objections, the certificate is issued. The marriage can take place in a church within the superintendent's district. The consent of the minister of the church must be obtained.

Divorced person wishing to marry in the Church of England

Where either party is a divorced person, a remarriage cannot, as a rule, be solemnized in the Church of England. However, this can be left to the discretion of the local church to exercise their own judgements. Times have changed and the church is changing with the times. However, this rule of non-marriage does not apply where the marriage has been annulled. Other stipulations to a Church of England Wedding are laid down in the law, as follows:

- the marriage must be in an unlocked church
- between the hours of 8am and 8pm
- two witnesses must be present

Other denominations and religions

If you belong to another denomination or religion other than the Church of England, you must first obtain permission from the civil authorities to marry. There are four ways of meeting the legal requirements, of which only one need be used:

- a superintendent registrar's certificate
- a superintendent registrar's certificate with a licence. This has a residence requirement of 15 days.

For those seriously ill or detained, special provisions under the Marriage Act 1983 and the Marriage (Registrar General's Licence) Act 1970 will apply.

Weddings for Jews and Quakers can take place anywhere or at any time under the Marriage Act according to their own practices. The marriage is solemnized by a person designated for the purpose.

Civil ceremonies

The General Register Office will issue a form 357, which provides notes on the legal formalities of marrying. Marriages in a register office require a solemn declaration from both bride and groom according to the civil form:

- that they know of no impediment to their union
- that they can call upon those present as witnesses that they take each other as lawful wedded wife or husband.

The two witnesses present then sign the register. The superintendent registrar and the registrar must both be present at a civil wedding, which can only take place in a registry office, except in very unusual circumstances where people are ill or otherwise confined.

Witnesses

All marriages, without exception, be they religious or civil, require two witnesses to the ceremony. The witnesses need not know the

27

couple. After a ceremony the witnesses sign the register and a marriage certificate is issued.

Marriages abroad

Generally speaking, a marriage that takes place in another country is recognised as valid in this country. However, all the laws associated with marriage in England and Wales must apply, such as the age restriction and the single person status. It is essential if a person intends to marry abroad that they seek legal advice to ascertain the status of the marriage in the UK.

Effects of a marriage

Being married confers a legal status on husband and wife. In general, questions of status, rights and duties concern the following:

Duty to live together

Husband and wife have a duty to live together. If one spouse leaves the other for good then an irretrievable breakdown has occurred (see next chapter on divorce).

Duty to maintain

Spouses have a duty to maintain one another. This extends to children, obviously, and becomes a particular problem on breakdown of marriage.

Sexual relationship

Husband and wife are expected to have sexual relations. Failure to consummate a marriage, as we have seen, can lead to annulment of a marriage.

Fidelity

Husband and wife are expected to be faithful to one another. Adultery is one of the main grounds for divorce.

Surnames

A wife (civil partner, Same sex married) can take her/their husband's surname but is not under a legal duty to do so. A wife's/partner's right to use the husband's surname will survive death and divorce. A husband can also take a wife's surname although this is unusual. Occasionally, couples will adopt both surnames. If a wife changes her surname to her husbands she can do so informally, simply by using the name.

However, change of surname must be declared to institutions such as banks and a marriage certificate must be produced.

Joint assets

The matrimonial home as well as family income become assets of a marriage. As we will see, a breakdown of marriage can lead to long and costly battles over assets of a marriage.

Common parenthood

Husband and wife/civil partner/same sex couple automatically acquire parental responsibility for the children of their marriage. If the couple separate the courts can alter the relationship between parent and child.

Marital confidences

Secrets and other confidences of married life shared between husband and wife/civil partner/same sex couple are protected by law. This is particularly relevant in this day and age where the tabloids invade the lives of people as never before. Married, and even divorced, persons can obtain injunctions to stop publication of confidential information.

Marriages of convenience

The laws surrounding such marriages have been gradually tightening up. Such marriages are seen as sham devices to get around UK Immigration law. In order to issue a person with an entry clearance certificate to enter the UK as an affianced person or spouse, the immigration authorities will want to be sure that:

a) the 'primary' purpose is to get married and that a separation will not take place after marriage and entry
b) that spouses intend to live together as husband and wife

c) if the couple are not already married that the marriage will take place within six months.

It also must be shown that parties to the marriage will settle in the UK.

Cohabitation

Despite people's perceptions to the contrary, there is no such thing as 'common law' relationships, i.e., people living together unmarried, as man and wife. As far as the law is concerned, they are two legal individuals. There is no duty to cohabit, no duty to maintain.

Regarding children, the duty of care usually falls on the mother. However, in the case of unmarried couples, both mother and father can enter into a parental responsibility agreement which should place them in a similar position to married couples regarding responsibility to children. If a couple who cohabit and have children do separate then there is a duty on the father (absent parent) to maintain the child until they reach the age of 17.

Effect on assets

The courts can decide what split will take place regarding assets of a cohabiting couple. This share is based on concrete facts of the individual's contributions. A live-in partner has no right to occupy the family home under the Matrimonial Homes Act 1973, in the event of breakdown of relationship. However, the law has tightened up in this area.

Taxation

There are important differences between the tax position of married and cohabiting couples.

These are as follows:

- cohabiting couples cannot take advantage of the taxation rules between husband and wife that ensure gifts between husband and wife are free of capital gains tax
- they cannot take advantage of the fact that on the death of a spouse, the other spouse inherits free of inheritance tax

However, as these rules change frequently you should refer to your local take office for advice. You should also take advice concerning Wills and Pensions.

Where the law treats cohabitees as husband and wife

There are certain areas where the law will afford the same protection to cohabitees as married people:

- Victims of domestic violence are entitled to protection whether married or not
- Regarding security of tenure, a couple who live together as husband and wife will be entitled to joint security whether married or not

- Certain DHSS benefits are available for live in couples. You should seek advice from the local benefits agency
- A duty to maintain the children of a relationship is imposed- irrespective of whether married or not
- Under the Fatal Accidents Act, dependant cohabitees, who have lived together for two years or more may be entitled to damages on his or her death.

Agreements

Cohabitees can enter into agreements to protect property and other assets in the event of splitting up. Married couples also do this.

At common law, a husband 'administered' his wife's property. In effect, a woman no longer owned property after she married. The law moves on thankfully! Today, property that a woman owned before marriage remains her own. If divorce takes place the question to be considered is whether the property has become an asset of the marriage. Each case will turn on its own merit. In view of the courts wide powers to determine what happens to assets after marriage, few couples enter into agreements (Pre-nuptial agreement being the most common). However, the wealthier the person, the wiser it is to enter into such an agreement.

Cohabitation agreement

When unmarried couples part, the courts have little powers to determine the split of assets. In relation to cohabitation agreements, there are problems under the law of contract. When parties enter a contract, both sides have to offer something towards the contract. This is called 'consideration' for the contract. In an agreement to cohabit it would be difficult to define consideration other than based on a sexual relationship. Nevertheless, it is wise to have an agreement as a basis, or structure, of the relationship when it concerns assets.

The law in Scotland

In Scottish law the minimum age of consent for marriage is sixteen and, unlike in England, no parental consent is required for 16–18-year-olds. All notices of intent to marry must be made to the district registrar, in person, in the district in which the wedding will take place. Neither party needs to live in the district and only 15 days notice is required. If either party is divorced from a previous partner six weeks notice will be required. Evidence that a previous marriage has ended will need to be produced.

Marrying a citizen of a foreign country

Foreign nationals may marry here providing United Kingdom legal requirements are met. Only one person needs to establish residency which must be in the district where the marriage is to take place, and only one notice of intent to the registrar or minister is needed. Nevertheless, the other party must be in the country on the day that notice is given even if they do not actually live here. If both parties are foreign nationals, and intend to return to their native countries, then it will be necessary to find out that the legal requirements of a UK marriage satisfy those of the native country.

If you are a British citizen marrying a foreign national, and your prospective spouse has only temporary leave to live here, either to study or work, or have medical treatment or for some other temporary purpose, marriage to you may not necessarily guarantee permission for your partner to stay permanently.

Civil partnerships

A Civil partnership is a legal relationship, which can be registered by two people of the same sex and heterosexual couples. The Marriages and Deaths (Registration etc) Act 2019 makes provision about the registration of marriage for heterosexual couples; couples within a civil partnership can obtain legal recognition for their relationship and can obtain the same benefits generally as married couples.

Civil partnerships came into force on 5th December 2005. The first civil partnerships registered in England and Wales took place on 21st December 2005. Civil partners are treated the same as married couples in many areas, including:

- tax and inheritance tax
- Employment benefits
- Most state and occupational pension benefits
- Income related benefits, tax credits and child support

- Maintenance for partner and children
- Ability to apply for parental responsibility for a civil partners child
- Inheritance of a tenancy agreement
- Recognition under intestacy rules
- Access to fatal accidents compensation
- Protection from domestic violence
- Recognition for immigration and nationality purposes

The registration of a civil partnership

Two people may register a civil partnership provided they are not already in a civil partnership or legally married, not closely related and both over 16 although consent of a parent or guardian must be obtained if either of them are under 18. Registering a civil partnership is a secular procedure and is carried out by the registration service, which is responsible for the registration of births, deaths, and marriages. A civil partnership registration is carried out under what is termed a standard procedure, which can be varied to consider housebound people or people who are ill and are not expected to recover.

The Marriage (same Sex Couples) Act 2013

The Marriage (Same Sex Couples) Act 2013 came into force on 17 July 2013 and allows same-sex couples the same right to marry as opposite-sex couples. Ceremonies will be able to take place in any civil venue and religious organisations will have the opportunity to "opt in" to performing religious same-sex marriages. However, the Church of England and the Church in Wales are specifically prevented by the legislation from conducting same-sex marriages. The new Act remains separate from the Marriage Act 1949, which allows opposite-sex couples to marry, although the provisions are largely the same and afford married same-sex couples the same legal status as married opposite-sex couples. The term "marriage" and "married couple" is now extended to include same-sex couples.

However, there are some differences between the provisions for annulment and divorce for same-sex marriages in the Marriage (Same Sex Couples) Act and those provided for same-sex couples in the Matrimonial Causes Act 1973.

One of the grounds upon which an opposite-sex marriage may be annulled is for non-consummation due to the incapacity of either party to consummate it or the wilful refusal of the other spouse to consummate it. Although a same-sex marriage may also be annulled, the non-consummation ground does not apply.

In obtaining a divorce, an opposite-sex spouse can rely on the adultery of the other to prove that the marriage has irretrievably broken down (however, note the provisions of the Divorce, Dissolution and Separation Act 2020 which reformed the divorce process to remove the concept of fault). The act was passed in June 2020 and came into force on 6 April 2022.

The definition of adultery is *"voluntary sexual intercourse between two persons of the opposite sex, of whom one or both is married but who are not married to each other"*. The Marriage (Same Sex Couples) Act has amended the Matrimonial Causes Act to add that *"only conduct between the respondent and a person of the opposite sex may constitute adultery for the purposes of this section."* A same-sex spouse would therefore be unable to obtain a divorce based on adultery (although any alleged infidelity with another person of the same sex could be used as evidence of unreasonable behaviour in support of a divorce application).

The legislation also makes some alterations to the Gender Reassignment Act 2004, as it will now be possible for a transgender person to remain married after changing their gender, provided their spouse agrees. Previously, an application for a Gender Recognition Certificate (to be recognised legally as a person of the opposite sex) had to include a statutory declaration as to whether or not the applicant was married or in a civil partnership, as obtaining the Gender Recognition Certificate (GRC) would have the effect of making the marriage or civil partnership void. Following the new legislation, a married person applying for a GRC may remain married if their spouse consents. Applications for GRCs will now have to include a statutory declaration stating where the marriage took place together with a statutory declaration from the applicant's spouse to say that they consent to the marriage continuing after the issue of a full GRC. If the spouse does not consent, a statutory declaration will need to be made by the applicant to say that their spouse has not made a statutory declaration consenting to the marriage continuing, and the marriage will be made void.

****

THE ENGAGEMENT AND ORGANISATION OF THE WEDDING

Chapter 2

The Engagement

The preliminary step, for a good many people, but not all, to getting married is to inform parents, relatives, and friends. After parents have been told of the (hopefully to them) good news it is then time to inform friends and relatives. This is normally done by a card.

Following this it is custom to announce an engagement in the local or national papers. This is done by the parents of the bride. The announcement should be worded according to the circumstances.

If the parents of the bride to be deceased then it is customary for the happy couple to insert an advertisement themselves. The newspaper that the advert is being placed in can advise on the wording as this will differ according to the marriage. A public announcement of an engagement should never be made if one of the couple is legally married. It is custom to wait until a marriage has legally ended.

Engagement party

If it is intended to have a party to celebrate an engagement, the bride's family will usually arrange this. However, it is important to do this within sight of COVID rules. At some point during the party the father of the bride will make an official announcement, giving a toast and welcoming the groom-to-be to the family.

****

Chapter 3

Organisation of the wedding

The bride is very involved in the organization of the wedding and a fair degree of responsibility will fall on the shoulders of bride and mother. The bride and mother will usually organise the following:

- arrange for both sets of parents to meet if this has not already occurred
- discuss the overall plans for the wedding with the groom and both sets of parents. Although traditionally weddings are paid for by the bride's father, it is common for both parties to share the costs where agreed as one person paying for all can be an unacceptable burden
- compile a list of friends and relatives to be informed and arrange the engagement party
- bride and groom-to-be select wedding attendants and inform them of their role
- draw up a list of guests to be invited
- draw up the wedding gift list with the groom's assistance
- draw up a budget for the whole event
- if necessary, arrange wedding insurance

- choose a venue depending on the type of wedding
- visit the registrar or minister depending on what is chosen, church or registry office, deal with the legal requirements
- book the photographer, transport, entertainment, flowers, wedding cake and acknowledge gifts as they come in
- advise the best man of anything specific about speech
- choose the grooms wedding ring
- arrange for a rehearsal of ceremony
- if appropriate (it usually is) arrange the hen night

The responsibilities of the groom

It is tradition that the groom undertakes responsibility for the legal aspects of the wedding, choosing his best man and the ushers. He will organize the honeymoon, organize clothing for the male members of the family, buy the wedding ring and make a speech. In addition, the groom will obtain the Marriage licence. The documentation, ring and church fees are then passed to the best man. The groom should also ensure that luggage is taken to the reception and that a car to take the couple away after the reception is organised.

The role of the father of the bride

The father of the bride will escort his daughter to court and will also escort the bride's mother-in-law on going out of the church

Following the wedding (known as the recessional). At the reception, he will make the first speech.

As mentioned, the father of the bride traditionally carries the burden of paying for the wedding. However, this is a matter between families and is now largely outdated.

The role of the bridesmaid

The Chief bridesmaid will be in charge and will look after the younger bridesmaids. She will assist the bride with her preparations on the wedding day. She will hold the bride's bouquet and looks after the brides wedding clothes when she changes.

Role of the ushers

The ushers seat people prior to the ceremony and hand out order of service sheets.

Toastmaster

The toastmaster is becoming more and more a fixture at weddings and will take over some of the duties of the best man. They will formally announce guests to the reception receiving line as they arrive, announce speeches, propose toasts, and announce the cutting of the cake.

****

THE ROLE OF THE
BEST MAN

Chapter 4

The Role and Qualities of a Best Man

A wedding is a well-organised event and it is the role of the best man to ensure that proceedings go smoothly. A best man's role is many and varied. The groom must be at the ceremony on time, one of the most important roles. Guests must be seated correctly and, after the actual wedding have to be transported to the reception.

At the actual reception, the focus is on the best man and his or her speech. It is the one that guests want to hear. A best man's speech is very important as this can make the occasion or can leave it flat. There are key tips on speech writing and presentation in the final chapter of this book. The main roles of the best man are as follows:

- Organising the stag party for the groom
- Ensuring the groom gets to the ceremony
- Acting as witness at the wedding
- Organising wedding photo groups
- Assisting guests in their journey to the reception
- Making the main speech at the reception.

It is very important that the best man plans ahead as there are a lot of things to cover. Whilst not everything is the responsibility of the best man, overall, the responsibility falls on your shoulders!

As with everything, a well laid out plan, put together as far in advance as possible, will prove to be a great help. Below is an example of a plan which will also show you the key times in which to do things.

1. Receive invitation to be best man	Can happen up to 2 years in advance but say within 1-year eriod.
2. Work with groom in choosing ushers	6 months before wedding
3. Start organising the stag party	3 months before
4. Review wedding plans with bride and groom go with groom to get fitted with suits etc.	3 months before
5. Finalise plans for stag party start work on speech	2 months before
6. The stag party happens!	1 month before wedding. Never night before.

7. Meet ushers, discuss duties, check groom has ring, finalise speech.	2 weeks before the wedding.
8. Wedding rehearsal happens, finalise wedding schedule, hire suits and finalise speech	1 week before wedding.
9. Last minute checks of everything!	1 night before wedding.

The above is a basic guide. It is up to you how you plan but, importantly, do plan. Essentially, the most important role of the best man is to help the groom. The best man will get involved in the wedding preparations, help choose clothes and any other accessories, arrange transport, collect the buttonholes, help choose the ushers. The best man will also organise the stag party and make sure that the groom survives the party and gets home afterwards.

On the wedding day itself, the best man should remain calm. Other people, especially relatives, will not be calm. On the morning of the wedding the groom must be correctly dressed and arrives at the church on time with all the relevant documents and the ring. The best man will look after the ring until it is used in the ceremony.

When at the church, the best man will stay at the groom's side, standing a little behind and to the right of him during the ceremony, so that rings can be handed over. The best man will escort the chief bridesmaid into the vestry to sign the register and will escort her out of the church after the service. The best man will also be responsible for making sure that all fees are paid.

Once outside the church, the best man will assist the photographer, making sure that everyone is in the right place at the right time when the photographs are taken. After the photographs, videos and whatever else is happening to ensure that a record of the wedding is in place, the best man will ensure that everyone is sent on their way to the reception, that transport is in place and so on.

At the reception

At the reception, if there is one, the best man may be asked to announce the guests as they approach the receiving line. He or she can generally help to ensure that everything is running smoothly by playing host, offering drinks, chatting to people, helping to make them comfortable, making introductions and helping people to their seats. This role of host is very important because at weddings, especially where people don't know each other, some people may feel uncomfortable. A wedding is an ideal forum for, on one hand, big egos to show off and play to the gallery and on the other for the less confident to feel a little scared of the whole occasion. This is where the qualities of the best man can be most needed.

The best man will usually introduce the first speaker, responds to the toast from the bridesmaids, gives a speech of his own and then reads out the congratulatory messages from people who have been unable to attend. He will dance with the chief bridesmaid and the bride and as many other of the female guests as possible.

Finally, when the married couple are leaving for their honeymoon, the best man will make sure that the car is at the door waiting to take them away, packed with their luggage and with all necessary documents in place.

The necessary qualities of a best man

The 'best' best man will be self-motivated and able to take the initiative and shoulder responsibility. Not many of us have all the qualities necessary to be a best man. However, it is important to raise awareness of the main qualities needed to ensure that the role is fulfilled and that the day goes off smoothly.

Well informed and briefed

During the period running up to the wedding, a lot will be happening and it is up to the best man to be as well informed as possible. There will be many things to achieve and many questions to answer.

It is of vital importance that the best man knows the format of the day and where everyone should be at a particular time. Regardless of how organised the best man is as a person it will be necessary to plan using a personal organiser.

Make sure that all aspects are covered and that they are laid out on a weekly and monthly basis. As the wedding gets closer then they will become daily tasks.

Level-headed and punctual

It goes without saying that a best man, having so much responsibility to ensure others enjoy the day and that everything works like clockwork, should be level-headed, calm in a crisis and punctual. Given that co-ordination is so important on the day, it is no good having as a best man someone who is hopelessly unpunctual.

Everything should be checked in advance to ensure that no obstacles are put in the way of smooth co-ordination. Everything is timed in advance or should be. Almost military precision may be needed on a wedding day.

Stay sober

Again, if the best man is responsible for ensuring that a wedding day goes off successfully, then it is no good drinking large quantities of alcohol to give Dutch courage. This can detract from the proceedings as people can detect very easily when a person has had too much to drink. It doesn't exactly engender confidence.

Tact

Tact is a crucial quality of a best man. Tact usually increases with a person's level of maturity. It is important to notice and deal with problems before they arrive. Problems can be anything from family arguments to people sitting alone, to the drunken buffoon annoying others.

Speechmaker

This is one of the most important elements of the best man's duties. Making a speech may be a good idea one year before the wedding but on the actual day it can be nerve wracking. We will be covering speeches in more depth later. The speech shouldn't go on forever. It should be around four to five minutes long and no longer. It is almost certain that the speech will be well received as everyone will be in a good mood. However, don't try to be too clever, don't attack people and be sincere and to the point. The best speeches are mainly the shorter ones and are not too difficult to put together and deliver.

****

Chapter 5

Organising a Stag Party

Before we discuss the details of planning the wedding, we will discuss the planning and execution (unfortunate phrase!) of the stag party. Again, the stag party should be organised with current government restrictions on gatherings of people.

The party

This entails ensuring that the party itself is organised. As we will see, this can range from a basic night at the pub to something far more elaborate, such as a weekend away in a European city, such as Amsterdam or Paris. It goes without saying that the more elaborate and complex the party the more responsibility that will fall on the best man. Trips away mean flights and hotels and nightclubs or other venues to book.

The stag guest list

This can be a tricky part of the whole operation. As far as possible, guests should be chosen for their ability to get on with others. A drunken night out can end in fisticuffs if the wrong people are invited. Usually, 20 is the maximum and a lot of thought should be given as to whom. In addition to the profile of the list, thought needs to be given as to whether all people can fit in comfortably with the plans. For example, if the groom has decided to travel abroad, can everyone afford it? This is an important consideration and should be discussed with guests, or potential guests, before issuing invites.

Letting other people organise the stag party

It could be that if enough money is available and the organising is seen as a headache, then employing a company to organise the party is the best option. There are numerous companies available in the U.K who will organise a stag do and the types and kinds of events that they will organise, from a weekend away to mountain climbing, are numerous. See the appendix for a list of companies, websites, and phone numbers.

The actual party

As we have seen, the best man ideally is a person who is highly organised. These organisational skills can be put to the test on the day of the stag party. Getting everyone together at the initial place of meeting is a key task at the outset. Making sure introductions are made is also very important. It is amazing how many people wander around without knowing each other during a stag night. This is down to weak social skills of organisers. Make sure that the place to meet is pleasant and that people can settle in. Avoid

60

places like railway station pubs. Try for more city centre or town centre venues. If the trip is abroad then make sure everyone meets in a hotel lounge or somewhere similar.

Go easy on the boozing before arriving at the destination as this can jeopardise the party.

Managing the drinking during the party is also important. People drink at different speeds and therefore will be buying drinks at a different speed. Either a kitty system should be organised or people pay for their own in small groups. A minor point but an important one.

Practical jokes

Practical jokes at the groom's expense are a feature of any stag night. Basically, a little gentle humiliation is in order. Practical jokes shouldn't be taken too far however, as this can cause offence. One of the least harmful ways is to spring a surprise such as a strip-o gram (if the audience is male or the opposite if it is female).

Recording the party

Make sure that a photographic or video record is available of a stag party. This party is very important and likely to be remembered, so it is important to have an adequate record which can be saved for posterity, in much the same way as the actual wedding day.

Making sure that the groom gets home

One of the most important tasks of the whole night is making sure that the groom survives without major trauma, such as fighting or being thrown into prison. Keep an eye on the groom and ensure that at the end of the night wherever you may be, he is tucked up safely in bed with no damage done!

****

PAYING FOR AND ORGANISING THE WEDDING

Chapter 6

Paying For and Organising the Wedding

As pointed out, although it is tradition for the bride's father to pay for the wedding, in these more enlightened (and economically straitened) times families will normally share the burden as much as they can. Traditionally though the following will shoulder expenses:

Groom
- The wedding rings
- Wedding clothes
- Legal and Church costs
- Bouquets for the bride and bridesmaids, corsages for the mothers and buttonholes for the best man
- Presents for the best man and ushers
- The present for the bride
- The stag party
- Transport to venue for himself and best man and to the reception for himself and the bride
- The honeymoon

Bride

- The bridesmaids' dresses and gifts
- The groom's ring and gift
- The hen party

The father of the bride

- The wedding dress
- Brides' mothers' outfit for the day
- The wedding present for daughter and future son-in-law
- All announcements, invitations, stationery and photographs and videos
- All flowers for different venues
- Transport to wedding venue for himself or bride, the bride's mother and bridesmaid and from wedding venue to the reception for himself and the bride's mother
- Wedding cake
- Insurance (if any)
- Overnight accommodation for close family if appropriate

Invitations to the wedding

These will differ depending on the type of wedding you are having.

See overleaf.

If the wedding is given by the bride's parent's.

Mr and Mrs

Request the pleasure of your company
    (name of guest)----------------------------------
                at the marriage of their daughter

                    to/with

        At Halesowen Registry office/Church

On Saturday November 4th 20 at 2.30pm and the reception after at

    Reply address   RSVP

If the wedding is to be hosted by both sets of parents you should change the wording accordingly. Likewise, if the wedding is to be given by the bride and groom. If the invitation is for a reception only the appropriate form of words should be used.

Alternative invitations

Of course, it is up to you how you word an invitation. There is no cast iron rule that you must follow the laws of convention. The invite should always reflect what you want as much as possible and not what others expect, although with large families this may not always be easy. As stated, large stationers and wedding shops will have different samples of invitation.

Preparing the guest list

Traditionally, the bride's mother draws up the guest list in consultation with the bride and the groom's parents. The main thing is to decide on the total numbers of guests for the wedding and draw up the list. Some guests will be invited to the whole occasion and some to only part. If you are having a register office wedding then only the wedding party will attend the reception. It is important when compiling the list to beware of any special needs of the guests. Maps should be provided with invites showing the location of the wedding venue and reception. When received, tick off acceptances and refusals so that your list is maintained and up to date.

The reception-*The receiving line*

Weddings differ in the extent to which they follow tradition. At some weddings you will have a formal receiving line. If this is the case, the person co-ordinating the receiving line should be asked to keep the reception room doors closed until after the newly-weds and their parents and the senior attendants are ready to receive guests. This may involve ensuring that a member of hotel staff to guide early guests into a lounge or waiting area and offer them refreshments until such a time as the receiving line is ready. The receiving line is made up of the brides' parents, the groom's parents, the newly-weds and their senior attendants in that order, starting with the bride's mother closest to the entrance.

Table seating plan

The top table

The top table will seat the bridal party and there are several plans to cope with different occasions. The most common plan is for nine people with the bride seated in the centre and the groom on her right, bride's mother on his right, then the groom's father and the chief bridesmaid/matron of honour.

This looks as follows:

Chief brides maid	Grooms father	Bride's mother	Groom	Bride	Bride's father	Grooms mother	Best man	Second bridesmaid

This is the conventional seating plan and sometimes it will not be possible to achieve this. It is up to the bride and groom to decide what they want on their big day. A table should be seated to reflect family but also considering situations where problems are likely to arise.

One such situation is where both natural and stepparents are present at a wedding. Alternatives can be discussed with the function co-ordinator when booking a wedding. Below is an alternative plan for where stepparents and natural parents are in attendance.

	STEP MOTHER	GROOMS FATHER	BRIDE'S MOTHER	GROO M	BRID E	BRIDE; S FATHE R	GROO MS MTHER	STEP FATH ER	CHIEF BRIDES MAID
BEST MAN									

This alternative seats all at the top table but puts a healthy distance between the parties.

Wedding speeches

For many people, weddings are the only time in their lives where they will be asked to give a speech. Wedding speeches are most often given by novices who suffer from nerves and self-doubt. However, this is one of the most important days in the life of newly weds and it is crucial that you make a good speech.

The form

It is usual to have three speeches, and all are toasts. The first toast is proposed by the bride's father, or a close family friend or relative. He or she proposes the health of the bride and groom. Next, the groom replies, and proposes a toast to the bridesmaids. Finally, the best man replies on behalf of the bridesmaids.

As with all things, time has changed the usual customs and women are now beginning to assert themselves and make a speech after the groom has finished. Also, best men are also joined by best women. Each of these speeches need to be prepared in advance and delivered as one would deliver any speech. The following are suggestions for each speech.

(See overleaf)

The bride and groom

The toast to the bride and groom should express happiness at the occasion and wish them both luck in their new life. It is customary to compliment the bride on her appearance and to compliment the groom on his luck. You may wish to add an anecdote from having known the bride so long, or you may have a funny story about the first time you met the groom. Finish by asking the guests to raise their glasses and drink to the health of the bride and groom. The things not to do when making a wedding speech

- Never make jokes about the bride or mother-in-law. This is pathetic and outdated
- Never make remarks which are in bad taste
- Avoid smut, innuendo, or references to past partners
- Don't use the opportunity to score points
- Keep in mind that this is the bride and grooms' special day, so only add to their pleasure.

The Bridesmaids

Next up is the groom, who thanks the proposer of the previous toast and in turn proposes the toast to the bridesmaids. The groom usually compliments the bride on her appearance and thanks her for consenting to marry him. He usually compliments on his good fortune on having found her. He thanks his best man for supporting him, and for working so hard to ensure that the day has run so smoothly.

Sometimes, the groom also thanks the bride's family for allowing him the honour of marrying her. However, this is increasingly seen as sexist and outdated. The groom, however, should at least thank the bride's family for accepting him in their home.

The groom then proceeds to tell a few anecdotes before he turns to the subject of the bridesmaids. He should compliment them on how well turned out they are and thank them for attending his wife so well. He will finish by proposing a toast to the bridesmaids.

The main event

The best man's speech is usually the highlight of the wedding. The audience is expected to laugh and the speech is usually timed at between five to ten minutes.

Start by thanking the groom on behalf of the bridesmaids. Add your compliments to both them and the bride.

The usual course of events after this is to say something about your relationship with the groom, and to recount some lively stories about your youth together. If you did not know each other when you were younger then tell a few stories about recent events. While it is expected that you will embarrass the groom slightly, it is important that you do not overstep the mark and ruin his reputation.

72

Other speeches

If the bride and groom take a decision to vary this format, they should tell everyone involved and work out who is going to propose which toast. If the bride wishes to make a speech, she usually takes the opportunity to propose the toast to the people who have made the wedding such a special occasion.

While you are quite at liberty to arrange for as many speeches as you wish, avoid allowing them to go on for too long. It is highly likely that alcohol, food, endless speeches and so on, will all have taken their toll.

See appendix 1 for sample wedding speeches.

Cutting the cake

The last part of the ceremony is cutting the wedding cake. After the speeches the best man (or toastmaster) announces that the cake is to be cut by the bride and groom. The couple will hold the knife over the cake and together make the first symbolic cut. If the cake is large enough, it is tradition for the top tier to be saved for later, for example for the first wedding anniversary or christening.

Display of gifts

It is traditional to display gifts at the bride's parents' home. However, a display can be arranged at the reception so that all the guests can view them. Each gift on display should have a name tag attached and should be arranged in order of what they are, i.e., crockery and so on. After the reception, the bride's mother should pack away all the gifts and store then safely until they can be delivered to the newlywed's home.

****

THE MAIN DECISIONS TO BE MADE BEFORE THE WEDDING

Chapter 7

Main Decisions Prior To a Wedding

Setting the date

Theoretically, there is nothing stopping people getting married when they wish. However, there will be constraints relating to the availability of venue and of personnel. For a wedding to be valid in law, the exchange of vows and of rings and signing the marriage register must happen between the hours of 8.am and 6 pm Monday to Saturdays, even if a religious ceremony happens before or after those hours or on a Sunday.

A Civil ceremony in a register office can be completed in 15 minutes. A religious ceremony can, however, take place any time anywhere, and last as long as is desired. It can take place in a field, on a mountain top or anywhere that is chosen.

As a rough guide, a marriage service in a church will usually take between 40 minutes and one hour depending on the minister's address and the length and duration of the hymns. If a communion is included then an extra 20 minutes or so should be added depending on the size of the congregation.

Civil ceremonies and church weddings

If both parties to a wedding are practicing members of a Christian faith, for example, and neither has been married previously, then it is highly likely that a church wedding will be chosen. Even if the couple are not regular church goers, getting married in church may feel right. If this is the case, it is first necessary to find out the name and place of your local church. You will need to call the church and speak to the minister or the priest and make an appointment to see him or her. This will involve both bride and groom.

Depending on when the wedding is planned for, the meeting may be either brief or longer to go into more detail. A further appointment will usually be made to sort out the details, the music, the Banns etc. The date will be entered into the church's diary.

If the bride and groom live in different parishes then both churches and priests/ministers must be visited. The couple will usually be invited to participate in marriage preparation classes and encouraged to join the congregation and attend church if they don't already. A Catholic priest would want to know about a non-Catholic partner's intentions for the future, whether there is going to be a conversion and what faith the children are going to be raised in. A minister/priest is entitled to refuse to marry a couple if they have reason to believe that they are not committed to the ideals of that particular church. The minister/priest will recommend a rehearsal for the ceremony at some stage close to the wedding.

All involved with the wedding (except for guests!) should be there for a 'dry run' which will help to calm nerves when it come to the real event.

Civil ceremonies

Many people, for reasons of personal belief and also for reasons of cost, or for reasons such as divorce, choose to marry in a register office.

In chapter 1 of this book, we discussed the different venues in depth. In order to be a legal marriage, only the civil part of a ceremony is necessary and the simplest form is that held in a register office. This will be held in the offices of the local Registrar of Births, Marriages, and Deaths in a room designated for marriages.

Music can be played during a ceremony; flowers can be brought in and readings can be made. The only element that is strictly forbidden is the religious element.

Most marriage rooms will seat around 50 or so, so it is possible to have a sizeable wedding. Now that more places are licensed for civil ceremonies it is possible to choose larger venues.

Almost all licensed places will offer a wedding package so the whole affair can be conducted at the same place. Obviously, costs will vary with what is required. At licensed venues other than the Register office, a Minister of religion, or one of them, may be prepared to perform a marriage blessing. Whilst not religious premises themselves, private licensed venues do not carry the same sort of restrictions as register offices.

Marrying outside the United Kingdom

There is an undeniable attraction to leaving it all behind and getting married on some tropical or sun-drenched Isle. Travel agents offer a wide range of packages to many places such as the Caribbean, Mauritius and so on. The travel and accommodation is arranged, as is the paperwork and formalities for the wedding. Travel agents will also advise what documents are needed, both before departure and at the destination.

Most of the trips are for about three weeks in length which allows time to obtain any necessary residential qualification necessary to get married.

This kind of holiday with all the trimmings can be expensive. However, if you compare costs to a full-blown church wedding, an average being around £16,000 it is usually a lot cheaper. It also compares favourably with a simpler wedding.

Planning the wedding reception

This element of a wedding is usually the biggest single task. It is also without doubt the most expensive part of the day. At one end of the spectrum many couples find themselves having to organise and pay for a meal at a hotel, wine and entertainment. It can become very expensive indeed.

It is possible to plan something smaller and less expensive, such as a cocktail or general drinks reception. After the wedding ceremony guests are invited to join the newly wed couple for drinks, a toast and canapés before they make their getaway.

This kind of function is fine if people's expectations are not that high. Another way of avoiding all the pressures of a full-blown reception is to hold the wedding ceremony later in the day and invite all the guests to an informal party later, with a light supper thrown in.

Some people, rather than hiring function rooms in a hotel, will put together their own receptions in a local hall or school or similar. For these you will have to arrange a licence for the consumption of alcohol at the local magistrate's court and organise your own entertainment. Overall, doing-it-yourself is hard work but it is an option and there are mobile catering firms who can assist.

Whichever way you choose to go, it is essential to check the venue out and to get some kind of reference if possible as you will pay the price on the day for a poor venue and poor service. Also, make sure you know what everything costs before you book.

As a rough guide to costs for a reception in a three-star restaurant/hotel:

- Reception drinks-£3 per head-£30 per head for a three-course meal-£17.50 for a buffet-£12 for a bottle of reasonable wine

- If you want to hire an up-market venue such as a stately home this will set you back from £2,000 upwards depending on where and what it is.

- A marquee for 50 people can set you back £1500 pounds. Compare and contrast this with doing things on a smaller scale, such as having a drinks party or hiring a community centre and you will have some idea of what the varying costs may be. If money is no real object, then make it a day and night to remember. If it is a consideration then scale down the operation. In no way does this detract from the day.

Choosing the menu

The venue should provide a sample menu(s) and wine list. A good hotel should offer choices from finger buffets to full course dinners with plenty of variety of other dishes such as hot or cold platters and vegetarian dishes. In addition, special diets should be catered for. Wine and other drinks should be provided with the meal. Also, if the budget includes it you should have champagne on hand for a toast.

Accommodation

Most hotels will offer rooms at special rates to hotel guests and will even, if asked, provide a bridal suite for the newly-weds. If the reception is not at a hotel and overnight accommodation is required then you should book early to avoid disappointment.

Attendants

Anything between one and six bridesmaids (maids of honour) is the norm. The bridesmaids are usually young single females (over the age of six) from the bride's family. If the bride does not have enough relatives, then she will first choose from the fiancé's family then from close friends. A married attendant is called a matron-of-honour. There is normally only one matron of honour and she will be the senior attendant. In addition to the bridesmaids' other attendants would be a flower girl, pageboy and a ring bearer. Adult attendants are usually assigned to look after the junior attendants.

What to wear

Bridal dress

Shopping for a bridal dress can be time consuming and expensive, depending on what you are looking for. The white bridal gown is the dress most associated with weddings but the range of styles and fabrics on offer nowadays is immense. A ready to wear dress will set you back from £400 onwards but a designer dress can cost thousands of pounds. Bridal shops will also have an alterations and cleaning service which may be an additional cost over and above the gown.

Hiring a dress

Hiring a dress may be a cost-effective solution for the day. Most companies hire a dress out several times and the first hire will be around 50% of the retail value with each time getting cheaper. These dresses are of a simpler design and are washable.

Made-to-measure

If you purchase a dress from a ready-to-wear retailer then it will usually be on a made to measure basis as they don't usually hold stock. The whole process can take up to several months so this is an element that you should plan early, five or six months beforehand if possible. In addition, you will have to have a clear idea of what you want and photographs might help.

It is very important that you spend time at this stage as getting the design right is crucial.

Bridesmaids and the Matron-of-Honour

Bridesmaids are usually dressed in a style and colour that compliments the bridal gown. As with the bridal dress, the dresses may be purchased from a ready-to-wear shop, hired for a day or made to measure. To hire a dress costs from around £100 upwards with made to measure and ready-to-wear from around £80. Again, the same timescales apply for purchasing, and the purchase of the bridal gown will determine the style and purchase of the bridesmaid's dress.

84

Dress for the men

As with the bridal dress, what men wear is dictated by the style of wedding. The choice of clothes, at the end of the day, is left to the couple, but it is normal to wear a lounge suit of some description. Morning suits are popular and most men's wear shops will hire them out for the day. To hire a complete outfit of trousers, tailcoat, cravat, gloves and hat will cost anything from £100 upwards. The groom and attendants should, if possible, arrange to hire their suits from the same outfitters who can also advise on style and will be consistent with what they offer.

Transport

Transport is a very important element of a wedding and requires meticulous planning. A car is the most common form of transport hired for a wedding. Cars can be very expensive to hire for a wedding, especially if you are hiring a Rolls Royce or Bentley or stretch limo. Sometimes it is better to make do with your own cars. A look in the vehicle or weddings section of yellow pages will reveal that almost any form of transport is available for weddings, and the prices will reflect the type of vehicle available.

Transport before the ceremony

Transport for the bride is very important, because the bride needs to get to the church on time (as do all others). Whether the marriage is at a church or civil venue there will usually be several weddings going on so it is important that times are kept to. Before you book the transport, you should at least go and see the company and view the vehicle. You should also confirm how the vehicle will look for the wedding, i.e., how will it be dressed and so on. The things that need to be considered before you make a booking are:

- How often will the vehicle be used on the day, as it could affect your times
- Is there a substitute vehicle in case any problems arise with the chosen one?
- Will the flowers used be fresh?

The vehicle should be arranged well in advance, at least half an hour before the wedding, in order to ensure that it gets to the venue on time. A second car will be needed for the bridal party. For a church wedding the bride's mother and also the attendants will be ferried to church in a separate car. Several trips may be necessary to ensure all are taken to the venue on time.

For a register office wedding, the bride and her father will need transport. The bride's mother traditionally travels alone. However, as with all other elements of a wedding, it is up to the couple to plan accordingly. The most important thing is that all parties travel comfortably, arrive on time and with dignity.

After the wedding ceremony

After the ceremony, the vehicle that transported the bride and other escorts to the ceremony will take them to the reception. It is usual for this car to carry out several trips from ceremony to reception.

After the reception

Most people who get married will leave the reception and go on a honeymoon of sorts. Transport is needed to take the newly weds away to their chosen destination. This can be achieved by using your own car or, if you have had a few too many, then the hire company that supplied the bridal car will also take the couple away. Of course, this will be included in the cost.

Organising photography and videos

Wedding photographers are usually expensive and need to be booked well in advance. You should try to hire one based on recommendation. If this is not possible, then you should ask to see examples of previous work. The photographer should be willing to take photographs at other venues than the wedding venue such as the bride's house. Obviously, the price will reflect this. The photographer will be at the civil venue before the first guests arrive and will take photos before the ceremony, usually of the main people such as the groom and the best man. The arrival of the bride and her father will be photographed and the walk up the aisle will, if

87

permitted, be photographed. The usual package of photography for a wedding will include:

- An initial visit to the wedding location to assess the potential for pictures
- A visit to the bride's home and reception venue if appropriate
- Up to 100 proof shots from which the final selection will be made
- A photo album
- The chance for others such as relatives or friends to buy copies at an extra cost
- Insurance

The cost for an experienced photographer will be between £500-£600. The more well known, the more expensive. Video recording of weddings is becoming very popular. The video company will work to a schedule like the photographer and they should be booked up well in advance. The costs of a video will, like photography, vary and can cost anything from £300-500 and upwards. Always ask to see previous work.

Arranging flowers

Wedding flowers can be purchased from most florists. They will advise on availability and wedding floral designs are usually chosen from a catalogue or the bride can provide a picture of her own design. Visit the florist well in advance. The most common order is for a bridal bouquet, sprays for the bride's mother and bridesmaids and buttonholes for the groom, the best man, the bride's father, and the ushers. There may well be extras for the wedding venue and reception venue and for the bridal car. The florist can also advise on appropriate flowers if allowed to see a picture of the dress. In this way they can co-ordinate arrangements.

Fresh flowers are usually favourite, although it is possible to get silk or parchment although these generally cost more. The time of year will make a difference to cost. The average expenditure is usually dictated by when the wedding is and what is available. The bridal bouquet is likely to cost upwards of £40, a bridesmaid's spray £30 and buttonholes £4 each. Depending on what you want, expect to spend on average £200 on flowers for the day.

The wedding cake

A wedding cake is normally chosen from a local baker who will estimate the size depending on number of guests. The baker will normally have a catalogue and types and sizes can be mixed and matched. The cake itself is usually either a fruit cake or can be a sponge cake. A mixture is preferable. The baker, or the venue manager should be able to supply a cake stand and a cake slice for the day. The overall cost of a cake should be between £100-£150 depending on specification.

The wedding stationary

Like the other suppliers, good stationers will have a catalogue of wedding stationary. Designs are pre-printed with different typefaces to choose from. Details of the wedding are usually sent to the printer several months before the wedding to ensure that there is enough time to cater for mistakes. A matched collection of stationary will include:

- invitations to the church or civil venue only
- invitations to the ceremony and reception
- invitations to the reception only
- reply cards
- orders of service
- table name cards
- cake boxes
- table napkins
- thank you cards

The average cost of stationary should be between £40-60. In addition to standardized stationary, it is possible to get personalized stationery from individual designers. Your budget will govern this but, on many occasions, couples wish to differentiate the invites and other stationary.

Fees for marriage

These will vary depending on where you get married.

Compulsory costs

There is a required legal fee for marrying in a church. In 2022 it costs £560 if you marry away from where you live and £512 if you marry in your home parish. This is set by the Church of England nationally and is the same for every church. This basic legal fee includes the cost of the vicar, the church, calling your banns, a banns certificate, the marriage certificate, lighting, and all administration. This required fee has ancient origins and ensures your church can maintain essential services like weddings, christenings, funerals, and all kinds of other ministries for you and your community.

The full table of fees can be found by visiting the Church of England site www.churchofengland.org

Optional extras

The statutory wedding fee doesn't include extras you may choose or decline, such as: -

- The support of a verger, who ensures the church is warm, clean, and tidy for your wedding and can help with handing out Orders of Service and hymn books etc. They can assist with disability access if needed by your guests and guide people to find their seats, toilets, or crèche if there is one. They can be indispensable in larger churches, freeing up the vicar to give their full attention to you and the wedding service.

- Additional heating in the church. The vicar will let you know if this applies to your wedding.
- Having an organist, choir, or bell-ringers – these extra staff will all need to be booked in advance. Sometimes, the church may ask for a deposit to secure these bookings.

Bear in mind that if your wedding is filmed, musicians like the organist can request an increase in their fee to consider professional performing rights. Check with the church what the local arrangements are.

- Church flowers – some churches have a local flower arranger who can help you with the flower displays in church.

Extra copies of the marriage certificate.

You do not have to have any of these extras, but many couples are keen to have at least some. If you choose them, they will cost extra. The costs for each will be at your church's local rate.

Affording the costs

Talk to your vicar early on about what the total cost of your wedding is likely to be. It is good practice for the church to provide you with an itemised quote before your wedding so that you can see exactly what you will be paying for.

Once the final church bill has been agreed, some couples are still keen to offer a donation to the church. Donations may help to cover things like administration and the upkeep of the building. While these gifts are very kind, you needn't feel under any obligation. If you're struggling to afford your wedding costs, or finding yourself in financial difficulties, it is worth mentioning this to your vicar as they might be able to suggest ways to help. If you need to borrow to pay for your wedding, why not consider using a local credit union? Credit unions offer affordable and responsible credit, and some will even offer special deals on loans for weddings.

Wedding insurance

As we have discussed in the introduction, wedding insurance is always taken out and any broker will provide you with a quote. A premium will set you back a minimum of £75 although costs will vary depending on the extent of cover. You may be asking yourselves, what do I need insurance for? It will cover the following:

- Loss or theft or damage to clothing whether purchased or hired
- Loss, damage, or failure of photographs
- Illness or death of bride or groom or parent of either
- Failure of supplier to provide goods or services
- Loss or theft or damage to wedding presents
- Loss, theft, or damage of wedding rings

Getting your wedding arranged

If you can afford it and cannot bear the thought of arranging your own wedding then you might want to employ a company who will arrange the big day for you. Most companies who do this will act as agents and will leave it to you to conclude arrangements with suppliers.

Wedding gifts

Many couples compile a list of desired gifts, although some prefer to avoid this. The list will almost certainly reflect the needs of bride and groom. Whatever the reason for the list it should be as long and as comprehensive as possible allowing those buying gifts to choose.

There are a few ways of organising a list, to ensure that the same items are not purchased twice. The bride might choose a shop with branches nationwide and pay a visit to a local branch to see if they can deal with the list. In this way it can be co-ordinated. The list is then circulated to guests who will order, the manager will check the list to see that it has not already been ordered and wrap and supply to the bride. If the item has been chosen a message will be given to the purchaser and another item chosen. An alternative to this is to manage the list yourself. A copy of the list goes out to every invited guest who will call the bride or her mother to discuss their choice. The bride and groom will usually give a small gift to each of the attendants as a personal thank-you. The gift should be personal to the recipient. Below is a sample wedding gift list divided into different rooms and items:

Items for the kitchen

- Baking tins
- Bread board/Bread bin
- Microwave
- Knife rack
- Knife sharpener
- Can-opener
- Carving dish
- Cheese board
- Chopping board
- Fondue set
- Frying pans
- Saucepans
- Kitchen knives
- Mixing bowls
- Scissors
- Spice rack
- Steamer
- Toaster
- Toast rack
- Trays

- Vegetable rack
- Wok

Obviously, you can compile a list of your actual needs from the above depending on what you already have, the same with the lists below.

White goods

- Cooker
- Dishwasher
- Freezer
- Fridge
- Washing machine
- Tumble dryer
- Vacuum cleaner

Electrical equipment

- Alarm
- Blender
- Bread maker
- Coffee maker
- Food mixer
- Hairdryer
- Iron and ironing board
- Juicer
- Kettle

- Pressure cooker
- Radio
- Hi-fi
- Television
- DVD recorder

Cutlery

- Butter knives
- Carving knives
- Fish knives
- Teaspoons
- Assorted cutlery

Crockery

- Cups and mugs
- Butter dish
- Plates
- Coffee pot
- Cream jug
- Cruet set
- Dessert bowls
- Egg cups
- Milk jug
- Sauce boat

- Serving dishes
- Soup bowls
- Soup tureen
- Teacups and saucers
- Tea pot

Accessories

- Bottle opener
- Carafe
- Coasters
- Corkscrew
- Decanter
- Ice bucket
- Table mats
- Napkin ring
- Wine cooler
- Wine rack

Glassware

- Beer glasses
- Liqueur glasses
- Wine glasses
- Tumblers
- Sherry glasses

Linen

- Bathmat set
- Bath towels
- Bedspreads
- Cushions
- Duvet
- Sheets
- Duvet cover
- Hand towels
- Bath towels
- Napkins
- Pillowcases
- Valance

Furniture

- Bedroom suite
- Cabinet
- Chairs
- Table
- Dining room suite

Garden

- Garden tools
- Garden plants

- Barbeque
- Garden shed
- Hedge trimmer
- Hose and reel
- Lawn mower
- Strimmer
- Wheelbarrow

Miscellaneous gifts

- Ashtrays
- Answerphone
- Bath rack
- Bath cabinets
- Scales
- Books
- Candlesticks
- Clocks
- Fax machine
- Linen basket
- Luggage
- Mirrors
- Ornaments
- Rugs
- Pot plants

- Shower curtain
- Sports equipment
- Stepladder
- Telephone
- Toolbox
- Towel rail
- Vase

The above lists are not totally exhaustive and the final list will depend on the needs and requirements of the couple.

And finally!

The honeymoon

Traditionally, the honeymoon is taken almost immediately after the wedding, although not always. Arranging the honeymoon is exactly the same as any other trip and, like all other elements of a wedding, can either be arranged for you or you can arrange it yourself. If you are going abroad or plan to go to a popular spot in the UK then arrangements will need to be made early. If you plan to go abroad then you may find, almost certainly will find, that the flights do not dovetail into your wedding times. This means, as with many couples, that a night in a hotel is required.

Weddings, as well as being fun, can be very stressful as the eyes of many people are on you-you are the centre of attention. For many people, several hours of this can be exhausting. It may well be advisable to book the initial night in a hotel, away from everyone but yourselves and unwind and prepare for the honeymoon proper. Don't forget all the usual if you are planning to go abroad, passports, inoculations etc.

****

THE BIG DAY-DIFFERENT CEREMONIES

Chapter 8

Different Types of Wedding Ceremonies

In this chapter we will look at a variety of wedding ceremonies, Anglican, Roman Catholic, Christian Scientist, Church of Scotland, Hindu, Muslim, Jewish, Pagan, Quaker and Unitarian This list is not exhaustive and any register office can advise you on where to get information concerning particular types of ceremony.

In Chapter 1 we discussed the requirements of getting married in the UK. In this chapter we will look at various religious ceremonies and how they differ according to the faith.

Anglican Ceremonies

In Anglican faith, the ushers will be the first to arrive at the church. They will know how to seat the guests and have enough orders of service and prayer/hymn books for everyone. In short, their role is that of organising the basics, to ensure that the ceremony gets off to a good start.

Seating is arranged so that in the front pew, on the right-hand side sits the groom and best man, with the groom's family seated alongside and immediately behind. The front pew on the left is reserved for the family of the bride and the bride's attendants. The guests will arrive 15 minutes before the service and they will be seated by the ushers-bride's family to the left and grooms to the right.

Close family of both bride and groom are seated at the front with guests seated appropriately from front to back.

After the ushers, the bridesmaids and bride's mother will arrive. After this, the bride will arrive led in by her father. The bridesmaids will assist the bride to make sure that her gown and veil are neatly arranged and secure. They will then take their places behind her, in pairs with the youngest first, and begin to walk up the aisle.

As the bride and father enter the church, they should give one of the ushers a signal to inform the minister or priest that they are ready. At this signal, the organist will begin to play the chosen music and the groom and best man will leave their seats to stand in front of the chancel steps waiting for the bride and her father.

On arrival at the chancel steps the bride will release her father's arm and the groom will stand on her right-hand side with the father just behind the bride. The best man stands on the groom's right. The bride will hand her flowers and any other items to the chief bridesmaid of matron-of-honour so that her hands are free for the ceremony. If there are no attendants, she will hand these things to parents or friends.

The minister or priest will begin the ceremony with a short address, reminding the congregation of the solemnity of the occasion and that it is a happy event for the families and for the couple. Guests will be guided by their order of service.

The priest/minister will ask bride and groom separately whether they will take each other as spouse, then will say 'who gives this woman to be married to this man?'. The bride's father will step forward saying 'I do' and will take her right hand in his and place it palm down in the minister's hand. The minister then places her hand in the groom's right hand and the symbolic gesture of giving away the bride is then complete.

With prior arrangement with the minister or priest this part of the service can be omitted as it is seen as old fashioned and irrelevant. It may also be that the bride has no one to stand with her in her father's role. The bride and groom now exchange vows and give rings. The best man will place the ring on the minister's prayer book. After the exchange of vows and rings the couple are declared husband and wife and are invited to kiss to seal the ceremony.

At this point, the bride's father will take his seat with the bride's mother in the front pew, likewise the best man will take his seat. The couple will now kneel at the chancel steps to take the blessing and after prayers the minister or priest will lead them to the altar. If there is to be a communion it will be made at this point. After this ceremony, the newly married couple, their parents, the chief bridesmaid or matron of honour and the best man now go into the vestry with the minister to sign the marriage register. The completed certificate is given to the couple. The organist will then perform for the congregation.

Leaving the church

The procession will form behind the couple as they walk down the aisle. If there is a flower girl, she will walk in front of the bride scattering petals as she goes. The pageboy and ring bearer (if any) will follow the bride and groom carrying the train followed by the best man and chief bridesmaid or matron of honour, then ushers paired with bridesmaids. The bride's mother walks with the groom's father and the groom's mother walks with the bride's father as they follow the attendants. As they are walking friends and family will follow in sequence from the front pews onwards.

If it has been agreed, the photographer or video crew can take photos and videos but this is usually not permitted within the church. After the ceremony the photographer will arrange guests for group pictures, with the help of the ushers, and take individual and joint shots of bride and groom. Group shots are then taken.

Blessing services

For those who have been divorced or are marrying for a second time and wish to have an Anglican service to celebrate the wedding in a church where the vicar will not solemnize the wedding, a service of blessing is an alternative option. In such a service, the couple will walk down the aisle together at the beginning, or if she has not been married before, the bride may be escorted to join the groom who is waiting at the altar, while the congregation are singing the first hymn. The couple will then make their promises in front of the congregation as they have already done at the previous civil ceremony.

Buddhist Weddings

Weddings under the Buddhist faith are very rare as there is no prescribed wedding ceremony. It is possible to devise an individual civil ceremony reflecting the couple's cultural traditions and for a Buddhist priest to undertake a blessing.

Catholic Weddings

Any marriages undertaken outside of the Church of England will require a licence. A couple must give notice of their intention to marry to a local superintendent registrar. The marriage itself can be authorised by a priest. If this is not the case then a registrar must be present.

If you want to marry in a Catholic Church you will have to visit the priest and discuss the intended wedding. In relation to the actual ceremony, if the marriage is between a non-Catholic and a Catholic then the mechanics of where you will get married and who attends to give blessing will need to be discussed.

If both parties are Roman Catholic, the wedding ceremony will usually form part of a full nuptial mass. The main elements of the service will cover the significance of marriage, a declaration that there are no lawful reasons why the couple should not marry, promises of faithfulness to each other and the acceptance to bring up children within the Roman Catholic faith.

The service begins with a hymn and a bible reading, followed by a sermon. The priest will then ask if there is any impediment to a marriage and calls on the couple to give their consent 'according to the rite of our holy mother the church' to which each person responds, 'I will'. The couple join right hands and call upon the congregation to witness the marriage and then make their vows to cherish one another. Vows are then exchanged, the priest will confirm them in marriage and the best man hands over the ring, which is blessed and given or exchanged, with the couple acknowledging them as a token of their love and fidelity.

In addition to the ring, the groom gives gold and silver to the bride as a token of his worldly goods. Once the rings are blessed, the groom places the ring first on the thumb of the bride and then on three fingers in turn. Prayers and nuptial blessings follow.

After the final blessing is the dismissal, whereupon the bride, groom and bridal party move into the sacristy to make the civil declaration and to sign and witness the register. If there is to be a nuptial mass the bridesmaids take their seats in the front pew.

For the nuptial mass, the couple return to the sanctuary. They then kneel and the bride is assisted by the groom. If Holy Communion is to be received, those taking it move forward at the
110

appropriate time, returning to their pews afterwards. When the mass comes to an end, the couple proceed down the aisle from the sanctuary, followed by the chief bridesmaid and best man, and then the other bridesmaids, pageboys, and parents before the rest of the guests.

Christian Scientist Church

If the minister of the Christian Scientist Church has registered with the appropriate local authority, then the Church is licensed for marriage ceremonies. However, as the minister of the church is not usually a registrar then a local registrar will need to be present at a wedding ceremony.

If the church is not registered then the marriage will take place at a local registry but a religious ceremony can take place at the church afterwards.

Hindu Ceremonies

In a Hindu ceremony, the bride will usually wear a red sari with the groom dressed in white. The ceremony is informal and the guests relax even during the ceremony and chat amongst themselves. As with other marriages, if the building in which the wedding is to take place is registered to hold weddings, couples should give notice of their intention to marry so that a registrar can attend the wedding. If a building is not licensed then a civil ceremony will take place beforehand. At the actual venue of the wedding, the family of the

111

bride will arrange a sacred place, covered with material and with flowers placed in the centre. The bride will arrive first and will be hidden until the groom and the guests arrive. As the groom enters, lights will be waved over his head and grains of rice are thrown to symbolise wealth and fertility. The groom will then take his place with the bride under the canopy and the ceremony will commence.

Humanist weddings

Humanist weddings eschew religion but generally wish for a wedding ceremony that is fulfilling and emotionally satisfying. Humanists have a national network of trained officers. They have produced a book called *Sharing the Future* which contains details of their approach. It also gives details on sample wedding ceremonies. You can choose to have a ceremony which incorporates your own beliefs without the religious element.

If you contact your local Humanist Association you can locate the nearest officiant. See useful addresses at the end of this book. You may, if you wish, choose a member of your family or friends to conduct the ceremony, which is simple and straightforward. The focus is on commitment, love, and respect for each other, as it is with all other ceremonies.

A humanist ceremony can take the following form:
- Welcome guests

- Readings by the couple, friends and family about marriage, love, and commitment
- Vows made by the couple to each other and children
- Exchange of rings or other tokens
- Readings and poems read by couple and family and friends about their future together

Jewish

In UK civil law, a Jewish marriage may be solemnized in any building, at any time of day, provided the couple have obtained the necessary legal documentation from the registrar. Jewish weddings are solemnized either in an Orthodox synagogue under the authority of the Chief Rabbi, or in a progressive synagogue where the civil authority appoints a marriage secretary who is responsible for the legal side of a ceremony.

For a couple to be able to marry under the Jewish faith both must be Jewish. If one is not Jewish, they must undertake a conversion prior to marrying. Jewish weddings usually take place on a Sunday, they cannot be solemnised between sunset on Friday to sunset on Saturday (the Jewish Sabbath).

At the wedding the groom and all males must wear hats and the bride a veil. In all Orthodox and most progressive synagogues the bride must keep her hair covered. Prior to the wedding, the couple may be requested to attend pre-marital counselling with the Rabbi.

The Jewish wedding ceremony

The groom will arrive at the synagogue with his father and best man. When the bride arrives, the groom is escorted under a chuppah (silk or velvet canopy, supported by poles). The bride is led into the synagogue on the arms of her father followed by bridesmaids and the mothers of the couple. The wedding ceremony commences with a blessing from the minister. After the ceremony has ended, the couple are left alone in the synagogue room before joining the festivities. At the reception the Rabbi will say grace in Hebrew before and after the meal, which consists of kosher food. At Orthodox wedding receptions, the men dance around in a big circle between courses, holding handkerchiefs so that they do not touch each other. The bride and groom are carried on chairs around the room. There is lots of singing and dancing.

Muslim weddings

A Muslim bride dresses in a heavily decorated gown and wears a lot of jewellery. Female guests have their head and legs covered. Again, as with all other marriages it will be necessary to ensure that all civil requirements are undertaken. This will involve a prior civil ceremony either in a mosque if it is licensed or at a registry office.

Under Muslim beliefs, a marriage is a contract, and not a sacrament, and thus any lay Muslim male may conduct a ceremony. Women are seated on one side of the Mosque with men on the other. The service commences with a sermon and is followed by a reading from the Koran. The bride and groom give their consent to marry and are pronounced man and wife. There are further sermons and prayers and then the party moves onto the bride's house.

The bride's parents will host a reception, at which guests of the bride bring presents. One week later, the grooms' parents host another reception at which the groom's relations and friends bring presents.

Non-conformist weddings

Non-conformist weddings will include Methodist, Baptist, Congregationalist, United-Reform and Assemblies of God faiths.

Their services are similar to those offered by the Church of England but they are more flexible and open to innovation. These churches generally need a registrar official to be present at the marriage, as they are not usually registered to conduct marriages.

Pagan ceremonies

Pagan ceremonies encompass New Age Hand-fasting to formal Druid Ceremonies. Pagans are very much nature based and honour equality and unity with nature. Hand-fasting is an old Anglo-Saxon word for an agreement between two people. The joining of hands is common in many wedding ceremonies. Many other symbols of marriage may be included in the ceremony, such as sharing bread and wine, jumping over a broomstick into a new life together and exchanging rings and tokens. Weddings are generally held out of doors and attended by a Pagan Priest or Priestess.

Druid marriage ceremonies are attended by a druid or druidess. Guests will form a horseshoe, within which the participants at the ceremony will form a circle. 'Four gates' on the four points of the compass divides the circle. Again, it is conducted outdoors.

The ceremony involves the celebrants calling on heaven and earth to witness the marriage before the couple make their vows. The party walk to the four gates, embracing the elements that it represents-fire, water, earth, and air. Vows and tokens (rings) are exchanged and a candle is lit. The couple walk around the circle to be greeted by those present as man and wife, before forming a central circle. Close family and friends make a circle around them and the remaining guests join hands to make a final circle of existence, before a final blessing.

Quaker wedding ceremonies

The Quakers (The Religious Society of Friends) can hold weddings at any time and place. The usual place is the Meeting House normally attended by either or both of the couple. Quaker marriages are a Christian commitment and Quakers, like the Anglican Church, can register their own ceremonies. Like all other marriages, the venue chosen for the ceremony must be licensed, otherwise a civil ceremony will also be required. Marriages where one or both couples are divorcees are allowed.

Couples are required to inform their local meetinghouse in writing advising of their intention to marry. A meeting is held between the couple and a group of men and women to discuss the forthcoming marriage and its implications. The service is simple, no procession, music, minister, or any other pre-planned element. The couple sit at the front of the Meeting House facing the congregation. The dress is formal but not as elaborate as Anglican wedding ceremonies. Wedding guests can stand and speak at any time. When the bride and groom feel that the time is right to exchange vows they will stand and do so. After they have made their promises, they will return to their seats and the meeting will continue until the elders shake hands to signify that it is over. Rings can be exchanged at any time. Everyone attending the ceremony will go on to the reception.

Single-sex partnerships and marriages

The Civil Partnerships Act 2004 and the Marriage (Same Sex Couples) Act 2013 sanctioned same sex partnerships and marriages giving couples the same rights as heterosexual couples. As mentioned, it is now also possible for heterosexual couples to have a Civil partnership. A religious element is allowed for same sex marriages, with permission from the church, and civil partnerships are civil ceremonies conducted in either a registry office or a place licensed to carry out wedding ceremonies. The format of a civil partnerships/Marriage Act 2013 wedding is the same as that of a heterosexual wedding with slight changes in the wordings of the vows.

Unitarian

Most religious denominations view marriage as a holy sacrament recognised by God. Unitarians view marriage slightly differently as a decision made by two individuals in relation to their own spiritual views and as a freely chosen act rather than a conforming act.

The Unitarian Church welcomes people from different faiths and those who have been previously married. The service itself must contain the legal wording required in all weddings in the UK, the rest of the service is completely individual and may be arranged between you and the officiating minister of that church. You are free to adopt any style that you want. A Unitarian Minister will be able to perform the ceremony at any building registered for solemnization of weddings. The service can be held elsewhere but a civil ceremony must take place first.

****

Chapter 9

Budgeting For the Overall Wedding

It is important, right at the outset, that you put together an itemised budget for your wedding. You should go through each item in turn and obtain quotes and estimates.

- Write them into your budget sheet.
- Remember that an estimate is not a firm quote
- Deal only with reputable companies.
- Once you are happy with a supplier check contracts and confirm all details and bookings.
- Pay deposits on time to confirm bookings
- Allow yourself a margin of 5-10% on costings.

Overleaf is a sample budget breakdown which will be suitable for all kinds of wedding. This format should be adapted to take in your own expenses over and above the main expenses.

See overleaf

COST CENTRE	QUOTE	DEPOSIT
CEREMONY VENUE		
CHURCH/REGISTER OFFICE FEES		
FEE FOR MINISTER/REGISTER		
BANNS		
LICENCE OR CERTIFICATE		
BELLS		
CHOIR		
FLOWERS		
MUSIC		
PERSONAL DONATION		
RECEPTION VENUE		
HIRE OF ROOMS		
DECORATIONS		
FURNITURE		
FOOD AND DRINK		
FOOD		
HIRE OF EQUIPMENT		
SERVERS		
DRINKS WITH MEALS		
DRINKS WITH TOASTS		

OTHER DRINKS		
BAR ATTENDANT		
HIRE OF GLASSWARE		
WEDDING CAKE		
ENTERTAINMENT		
MUSIC OR DJ'S		
BRIDES OUTFITS		
DRESS		
HEAD DRESS		
TRAIN		
SHOES		
UNDERWEAR		
HOSIERY		
JEWELLERY		
GOING AWAY OUTFITS		
BEAUTY TREATMENTS		
HAIRDRESSER		
MAKE UP ARTIST		
PERFUME		
BRIDES MAIDS/PAGEBOY OUTFITS		
CHIEF BRIDESMAIDS DRESS		

BRIDEMAIDS DRESSES		
SHOES		
HOSIERY		
CLOTHES-GROOM/BEST MAN		
SHIRTS		
SHOES		
BEST MANS SUIT		
GROOM SUIT		
USHERS SUITS		
USHERS SHOES/SHIRTS		
FLOWERS		
BRIDES BOUQUET		
CHIEF BRIDESMAIDS BOUQUET		
BRIDEMAIDS BOUQUET		
BUTTONHOLES		
BRIDES MOTHERS CORSAGE		
GROOMS MOTHERS CORSAGE		
CHURCH FLOWERS		
RECEPTION FLOWERS		
RINGS		
BRIDES RING GROOMS RING		

TRANSPORT		
PHOTOGRAPHER		
MISCELLANEOUS		

****

Useful addresses and Websites

Addresses for copies of documents such as birth certificates etc.

General Register Office for England and Wales

Certificate Services Section

General Register Office

PO Box 2

SOUTHPORT

PR8 2JD

Tel: 0300 123 1837

General Register Office for Northern Ireland

Colby House

Stranmillis Court

Belfast BT9 5RR

0300 200 7890

National Register Office for Scotland

The General Register Office for Scotland (GROS)

New Register House-3 West register Street

Edinburgh Scotland EH1 3YT

Phone: 0131 314 4411

General Registry Office Guernsey

Market Building

PO Box 451

Fountain Street-St Peter Port

Guernsey GY1 3GX

Tel: 01481 222800

Addresses for civil and religious ceremony information.

Marriage Care

www.marriagecare.org.uk

0800 389 3801

Celtic ministers

www.Paganfed.org

The Foreign and Commonwealth Office

www.gov.uk/government/organisations/foreign-commonwealth-office

Humanist ceremonies

British Humanist Association

1 Gower Street

London WC1E 6HD

0207 324 3060 www.humanism.org.uk

Jewish ceremonies

Jewish Marriage Council

23 Ravenshurst Avenue

London NW4 4EE

0208 203 6311 www.jmc-uk.org

Quaker ceremonies

Quakers (The religious Society of Friends)

Friends House

173-177 Euston Road

London Nw1 2BJ

0207 663 1000 www.friendshouse.co.uk

Weddings in Scotland

www.visitscotland.com/about/scottish-weddings

Single-sex unions

One Body One Faith

www.onebodyonefaith.org.uk

Unitarian ceremonies

Unitarian Church

Essex Hall

1-6 Essex Street

London WC2R 3HY

www.unitarian.org.uk

0207 240 2384 info@unitarian.org.uk

Other addresses

Family planning
The British Pregnancy Advisory Service

www.bpas.org

03457 30 40 30

The Brook Advisory Centre

www.brook.org.uk

Honeymoon

The Association of British Travel Agents

www.abta.com

Information Services

Photography

The Society of Wedding and Portrait Photographers

The Societies of Photographers,

Clwyd Chambers,

Clwyd Street,

Rhyl,

Denbighshire, LL18 3LA,

Tel 01745 356935

www.swpp.co.uk

The Guild of Photographers

https://photoguild.co.uk/

****

Seven popular wedding planning websites.

Rock My Wedding

Rock my wedding is one of the UK's most popular wedding websites. It is dedicated to everything unique about the wedding world. In particular, it is a one-stop site packed with information. www.rockmywedding.co.uk

Guides for Brides

Guides for Brides is a wedding website that was launched in 1995. It is full of information for any couple looking to arrange their wedding day. www.guidesforbrides.co.uk

Bridebook

Bridebook is a wedding website designed to take the confusion out of wedding planning. www.bridebook.com

Hitched

Founded in 1997, Hitched has helped couples prepare for their weddings for over two decades. The wedding website chiefly prides itself on covering virtually every aspect of wedding planning. www.hitched.co.uk

Confetti

If you need inspiration about how you want your wedding to look and feel, Confetti features a variety of excellent list articles offering advice on topics such as how to plan your wedding on a budget and what sorts of flowers to buy for the big day. It also hosts an online shop where you can pick up small bits and pieces for your wedding. www.confetti.co.uk

UK Bride

UK Bride is a wedding website with a number of helpful resources. Above all, a database of wedding venues and inspirational articles. There is a forum for members to discuss their wedding ideas. www.ukbride.co.uk

Wedding Planner

Wedding Planner, allows users to search for their perfect locations and suppliers from a vast database. www.weddingplanner.co.uk

****

Appendix 1

Sample Wedding /Civil Partnership Speeches and Toasts

As we have seen, a lot of work goes into organising the big day. However, one very important area still left is that of the various speeches that will be made at the reception. It is important to be prepared and for those participating to have their speeches rehearsed and ready. The following 5 speeches are covered, in this order, which is the traditional order at the reception:

Father of the bride
Bridegroom
Best Man
Bride
Maid of Honour

When looking at these speeches you should remember that they are for guidelines only and you can pick and choose themes drawing ideas from the speeches and adapt them to suit the occasion, including same-sex marriages and civil partnerships.
Speeches generally

Father of the Bride or brother/sister or friend of the family.

The opening speech by either the father of the bride, or in his absence a member of the family or a friend should contain within it:

- Thanks to the guests for coming and participating in the special day
- Thanks to everyone who have contributed to the cost of the wedding
- Compliments and praise to the bride and welcome to her new husband and family
- A toast to the bride and the groom

The first speech below represents a typical speech delivered by the father of the bride.

Example speech-Father of the bride

A very good afternoon, ladies and gentlemen, I'm David and I have the undoubted honour of being the father of this blushing bride. However, I'm fully aware that my main function this afternoon is to warm you up, the audience, for the star performers who will speak later.

Most of you will know of Emma's interest in fashion so I thought I would try to make my speech like that well known item of fashion clothing, the mini skirt - short enough to be interesting and long enough to cover the essentials.

Today is, of course, a celebration, but not just of the love that has united Emma and Phillip in their marriage today, but also of the families that have created, moulded and influenced the lives of these two special people. So, my wife Sheila and I would like to

134

extend a very warm welcome to Phillips parents Lorraine and Arthur and to relatives and friends of both families.

A special welcome also to those who have travelled some way to be with us today. We have people from Portsmouth, Nottingham, London, and Birmingham.

Thank you all for joining us in celebrating this very special day.

Looking back, I clearly remember another very special day for Sheila and I, on a Sunday just 10,302 days ago when I witnessed the birth of our first child, Emma. Well, that seems like only yesterday. I have many memories of her as a baby. I've seen her wet herself and crawl around on the floor but I think that's enough about her 18th birthday.

There have been many memorable days along the way. Emma having acute appendicitis in France on, little did we know at the time, Phillip's birthday, in 2005. This will never be forgotten.

Her sleepwalks are legendary - two stand out in particular. The first was the time she woke Sheila at 3 am to get her to come to Emma's room to sort out the mouse that was in there. Chris stayed and talked to her only to realise after a while that Emma was asleep. Then there was the time she woke us up to say that burglars had telephoned to say that they were about to break-in - again whilst she was asleep!

But warmer memories are plentiful such as -

- -her wearing a hat for all of the three weeks we holidayed in America in 2014.
- -the time she chose to sit down in Lake Cosenostra,
- -her playing against Wolverhampton Wanderers - the ladies' team,
- -completing a half marathon, and, of course,
- -her degree success in 2016.

As I accompanied Emma here today there could not have been a prouder man and as we walked side-by-side I thought, and I'm sure you'll agree, that Jodie looked stunning ... and Phillip, well he looked absolutely stunned!

Of course, fathers are naturally biased where daughters are concerned, but in Emma I see an independent, intelligent, beautiful young woman, a daughter to be truly proud of. A daughter who, throughout her life, has always been ready to face a challenge. Some would say, however, that she's about to face her biggest challenge of all...which brings me to the other half of this partnership.

Seriously, when his child is young, a father sometimes contemplates the image of the man his daughter will marry. Will he be kind - intelligent - thoughtful - generous?

Just over 5 years ago Emma introduced us to a young man with DREADLOCKS -. Phillip.

We are delighted that Emma now has a husband with all these attributes and more.

During the time we've known Phillip we've come to realise how much he means to Emma. When you see how gorgeous Emma looks today, it proves the one thing I've always known about Phillip – he is clearly a man of vision...Occasionally blurred, sometimes double, but nonetheless a man of vision - and they have been fortunate to have found each other. So it's a pleasure, Phillip, to formally welcome you into our family.

I was struck by his thoughtfulness during a conversation we had one Monday after work in The Bay Horse in June last year. Phillip asked for my permission to propose to Emma. He had clearly given the matter a great deal of thought and Emma was at the centre of everything he said.

An example of that generosity I mentioned just now was shown last November when Phillip treated me to a day out. A trip to Twickenham to see the Barbarians play Australia - alas we, well most of us in the room, lost 11 - 60. To return the favour I treated Allun to an afternoon at The Mem to watch Bristol Rovers play Bradford City - somehow, we won 2 - 1. I probably got the better of that exchange but Phillip's done very well today, hasn't he?

And perhaps the ultimate compliment comes from Emma's brothers Roger and Robert who think he's sound.

Now, it's customary on these occasions for me to offer the happy couple some worldly advice on marriage. As is the fashion

137

today, Emma and Phillip have already set up home together and so already know a lot about each other. I am delighted that both are making very good progress in their chosen careers yet also find time to do lots together, for example the surprise birthday treat a day trip to The Peak District and holidays to Tenerife, Morocco, and Canada.

So, Phillip, remember there is no challenge in a marriage that can't be overcome by one or more of the following:

Ok, I was wrong, ok, you were right, Yes Dear And the most important - OK love! Just buy it!

From recent personal experience I would say don't make assumptions, for example - Sheila was enjoying a glass of wine one fine summer's evening on the patio with me. I heard her say, 'I love you so much. I don't think I could ever live without you'. Wow, I thought and asked Sheila, 'Is that you or the wine talking?' She replied, 'It's me...talking to the wine'.

Finally, there is a saying, which goes something like 'Happy marriages begin when we marry the ones we love, and they blossom when we love the ones we marry.' So, Emma and Phillip may your marriage be a truly happy one, may it begin with an unforgettable honeymoon in America, and may you both have a long and wonderful life together.

Ladies and gentlemen would you please be upstanding and raise your glasses for the toast - The Bride and Groom.

The Father of the Bride Wedding Toast

The Father of the Bride will be the first of the speechmakers to raise a wedding toast.

At the end of his speech, he will lift up his glass, say a few words then raise a toast the Bride and Groom. It is traditional for his wedding toast to include sentiments of a healthy and happy life for the newlyweds, although there are no restrictions whatsoever on what else the Father of the Bride has to say.

The following is a short example of a typical Father of the Bride wedding toast:

"Now I invite you all to raise a toast to my beautiful daughter and my son-in-law. May they live a wonderfully healthy life together and enjoy many, many years of happiness.

To the Bride and Groom."

Bridegrooms' speech

The Groom's wedding speech is made on behalf of himself and his Bride and uses the opportunity to personally thank the people involved in the wedding preparations. In his speech, he will toast the Bridesmaids and thank them for a job well done and will thank his groom's party for their support throughout. The Groom's speech should also include a special thank you to his parents and maybe even include some special memories with them.

Any family members or friends who could not attend the wedding should be remembered in the Groom's wedding speech.

As the Groom's speech comes before his Best Man's speech, he may wish to incorporate a few jokes and memories about his right-hand man! Another entertaining and sentimental part of the Groom's speech is when he shares his first encounter with his wife and how his life has changed because of it!

Example speech Bridegroom

Finally, after eight and a half years, I can say this... on behalf of my wife and I, I would like to thank you all for coming, for sharing our special day with us, for your presents and your love.

I would like to thank Fred for his kind words. I know I'm supposed to be responding for my wife and I, but she's more than capable of speaking for herself, as she will prove in her own speech after mine.

I'd like to thank my Mum and Dad, Henry and Sheila, and Fred & Maggie, not only for their financial assistance, but also for their support and guidance when needed, and for leaving us to our own devices and letting us do "our own thing" when we needed to.

We'd like to show our appreciation with some flowers for each of them (flowers for mums and Maggie)

When thinking about what to put in my speech I looked at a variety of sources, but I always ended up, back with the Big Man.

The true light,

My guiding spirit,

The one who has a following of millions,

Homer Simpson.

When asked what marriage is like he responded:

"Marriage is like being married to your best friend, and he lets you play with his boobs".

Everyone who knows me well will understand exactly where Homer and I, are coming from with that one.

I then considered writing a poem for today, describing all the loves of my life, so everybody would know how truly happy I am, but unfortunately, I couldn't get Sophie, Harlequins, Guinness and Lardy Cake to rhyme!

Then during the research for this speech I came across a short verse written by Wilfred A Peterson called "The Art of Marriage".

I would like to read this now to Sophie, but I feel the sentiments apply equally to us all.

The Art of Marriage

A good marriage must be created,

In the art of marriage, the little things are the big things.

It is never being too old to hold hands,

It is remembering to say, "I love you", at least once each day,

It is never going to sleep angry,

It is having a mutual sense of values and common objectives,

141

It is standing together, facing the world,

It is forming a circle of love that gathers in the whole family,

It is speaking words of appreciation and demonstrating gratitude in thoughtful ways

It is having the capacity to forgive and forget,

It is giving each other an atmosphere, in which each can grow,

It is finding room for the things of the spirit,

It is common search for the good and the beautiful,

It is not only marrying the right partner,

It is being the right partner.

Sophie, in front of all our friends and family I promise I will try my best to practice this art.

So, to my new wife, it doesn't seem five minutes since I was proposing to you on the beach, under the stars, proposing twice to you as it happens, as you made me do it again, "because it was over too fast the first time".

I'm so happy to be married to this beautiful, stunning, good looking and talented woman. I suppose every groom thinks his bride is the most beautiful in the world, and today that's how I feel.

I'm completely overwhelmed at how fantastic she looks and feel hugely privileged that's she chosen to be my wife. I have been completely misled by the girls as to what Sophie would look like today, so much so, that she looks a million times more lovely than I could possibly have imagined.

Thank you for making this the best day of my life so far, and I hope that every day will be as happy as today……. just less expensive.

Sophie has promised not to change after we are married. So, I'm looking for to more tact, more diplomacy, and many, many more made-up songs around the house.

When I finally got round to telling Sophie what I do for a living, I was rather surprised to learn that not only did she knew what a quantity surveyor was and what I do for a living, but also that her

Dad and Granddad were ones as well, and not just QS's but Partners in their own firm! The first meeting with Ian was a tad daunting for a newly qualified surveyor and boyfriend to say the least!

I'd also like to thank Claris, Katie and Jonathon for delivering the readings so eloquently, and to David for videoing the ceremony and these speeches.

I'm quite a superstitious sort of bloke, and I've noticed over the last week or two some very good omens for this day and for this marriage. Last week I saw a shooting star and made a wish, last Monday I saw a double rainbow, today Southampton are above Portsmouth in the football league and to cap it all Harlequins beat London Irish today and are still unbeaten and at the top of the Rugby Premiership!

Now to the "Al's", Alistair's, and Alan. Thank you both for organising the stag do, which I'm told I enjoyed enormously.

Thanks to Alistair for ushing and for being my mate, it is very much appreciated (Alistair's present).

I've known Alan since we started college together some nineteen years ago, we've had some very good times together which I'm sure he'll tell you about shortly, if he can actually remember them. I'd sincerely like to thank him for being my best man today. (Alan's presents)

I should perhaps just mention that Alan suffers from a rare medical condition, which, makes him prone to embellishment and suffer delusions about fairies. He often invents the most fanciful stories, which he sincerely believes to be true. I hope you bear this in mind when he stands up to speak after Sophie.

Sophie and I would like to thank the three bridesmaids, Susan, Katy and Lauren. You've all been terrific and done a great job today and over the last few months. I'm sure you'll all agree that they all look beautiful. We'd like you to except these gifts as a token of our appreciation and as a reminder of your involvement today (presents)

And finally, a toast to our three lovely, helpful, and very patient bridesmaids,

The Groom's Wedding Toast

Traditionally the shortest of the three main speeches, the Groom's wedding speech should always be concluded by the raising of a toast to the bridesmaids. As with the Father of the Bride toast there are no set guidelines or rules, but it is advised that any Groom's wedding toast doesn't look to place too much emphasis on how beautiful the bridesmaids all look, just in case his new wife decides to take offence!

The following is a short example of a Groom's wedding toast:

"May I take this opportunity to thank each and every one of the Bridesmaids here today. You've been a great help to my new wife and I and we are both very appreciative for all your efforts. So if everyone could please join with me and lift up their glasses and raise a toast - to our bridesmaids."

Ladies & gentlemen...the bridesmaids

The Best Mans Speech

The best man's wedding speech is usually the most eagerly awaited of all the wedding speeches. Traditionally the best man's speech is the last which gives the groom the chance to get one or two quick jokes in at the best man's expense. This can be a dangerous game as the best man can always have a couple of extra stories for his speech up his sleeve if he feels the need for revenge.

When preparing your best mans speech remember to think about your audience, find out the mix of people attending and try to weave something for everyone into your speech. Aim for your speech to be about 5 minutes but no more than 10 minutes. You will find that your best man speech takes longer when you deliver it on the day once all the laughter and cheering is factored in.

The best man's speech will contain within it:

- Thanks to the groom for his toast to the bridesmaids
- Comments on the bridal couple, particularly the groom
- The reading of any messages from absent friends and relatives
- The toasting of the bride and groom

Best man-Example speech

Before I undertake the customary duty of giving Martin an uncomfortable few minutes it is part of the official duty of the best man to thank Martin on behalf of the bridesmaids, Lotty, Gemma and Claire for his kind words and for having them play a part of this special day. I have to say they all look wonderful and have done an excellent job. Indeed, they are only eclipsed by Sue herself, who, I'm sure you'll all agree, looks absolutely stunning.

It is a great privilege to be asked by Martin to be his best man. He has quite generously returned the favour that I asked of him 6 years ago, during which Martin took the opportunity to make lots of cheap jokes at my expense, so I now have the right to reply.

I suppose the first thing the best man should explain is how he knows the groom. Well, being his identical twin, we first met long before we can both remember, so we are very close. There's nothing I wouldn't do for Martin, likewise there's nothing Martin wouldn't do for me, in fact we spent most of our time doing nothing for each other.

I will start at the point of our early life as toddlers.

Growing up together in those early days, I am proud to say that I was an angelic child, no trouble to anyone, but the same could not be said of Martin. He showed no respect to his elder twin brother. I became an innocent victim of his loutish behaviour. "Lloyd, flush your socks down the toilet" he used to say. And under duress I did.

But that lout grew up into the well mannered and well-presented individual we see sitting here today. Martin has matured.

For instance, I can tell you that Martin is very well read - he has after all read all 45 of the Mr Men books from cover to cover. In fact, at the age of five, whilst living in Australia, Martin had a great idea to wander off into the dense, wild outback behind our house to look for Mr Jelly, whom he had read lived in the middle of a forest. He convinced me to go with him and we got terribly lost. By the time we had found our way home, there were lots of tears. Not for the fact that he had been lost in a forest, but that Martin never found Mr Jelly's house.

Regarding Australia, it was there that Martin began a love affair which still lasts to this day. McDonalds. Age six, we were ever so excited to make our first visit to McDonalds and the great thing about this place was the kids' playground - it was like a mini-theme park - things to climb, things to slide down, things to spin around in all for the enjoyment of children who had just scoffed their face with burgers and fries. It was whilst Mum, Dad, Verity and I were sat inside the restaurant that Martin, having just stepped off the swings, appeared the other side of the window. knocking loudly so that everyone in the restaurant noticed him. My parents played along and waved back...until Martin, in full sight of everyone tucking into their lunch, brought up his fast food as quickly as it had originally gone down, all over the windowpane. Suddenly my parents stopped waving and momentarily tried to pretend he wasn't theirs, although sadly as Martin's twin was sat with them at their table, they couldn't fool anyone. The waitress gave them some reassurance. "Don't worry guys, that happens here all the time."

His love of fast food however never stands in the way of his enjoyment of sport. Martin usually waits until half time to get off the sofa to ring for a pizza. Some of you may be aware of his passion for cricket. What many of you don't know is that his interest in the sport was borne during his time at school. Martin is a modest man - well, that's what he has insisted I tell you - so his cricket achievements are little known. But today I can reveal that at school, Martin SCORED more runs than any other person in the entire cricket team - that was because he was always 12th man putting up the numbers the scoreboard at the pavilion.

After school, Martin went on to study environmental science at Kings College London. I am told by his friends many of whom are here today that Martin had a natural flair for the subject. They tell me that no matter how remote a place Martin was sent away on field trips, he could gauge and interpret the direction of the wind, the contamination of the soil and the pollution of the air to produce an accurate assessment of where the nearest local pub was to skive off to have a pint of lager and a packet of crisps.

But Martin had to fund his extra curricular activities. Being a student with far too much time on his hands and always in need of an extra few quid, Martin decided to exploit a promotional campaign at Selfridges, the famous department store on London's Oxford Street. The deal was that customers were entitled to a voucher if they purchased an item from all seven floors. Martin managed to get round the store and buy small items that came to the grand total of 37 pence. It was an all-time record amongst his fellow students. Selfridges had no choice but to pay out the voucher, which Martin then redeemed for cash. What's more impressive or should I say sad is that he did this seven times in one day to walk away with a hard-earned voucher. Unsurprisingly, Selfridges ended their promotional campaign rather abruptly.

Although Martin studied environmental science, I began to doubt his true commitment to the green cause when he purchased his first car after leaving university, a Volkswagen Beetle. Now, I'm not sure what year the Beetle was made, though I believe the front of the car was made in the early nineties and the rear of the car some years before. Martin spent hours in that car, usually trying to

149

get it to start. It was the only vehicle that you wouldn't use a traditional road atlas or street map to navigate your journey. Martin's Beetle was so economically inefficient and powerless that he had to plot his routes using an ordinance survey map to make sure that his entire route was downhill. With careful planning, Martin could achieve this, and the only flaw was making the return journey home by the same route.

Being Martin's older twin, by a whole five minutes, I realise Martin that you have now reached the age that I was when I started this speech and with that you will gained the maturity and wisdom that I had back then. So, this is probably a good time to for me to show some respect.

Joking aside, I want to say what a privilege it is today to be your best man. I couldn't wish for a better brother and how much you mean is impossible to put into words. The whole family is proud of you Martin, and we are all thrilled to see you marrying your beautiful bride sue today

So, it now gives me immense pleasure to invite you all to stand once more and raise your glasses in a toast for Martin and Sue. We wish them well for the future. To love, life, laughter and happily ever after.

Martin and Sue.

The Best Man's Wedding Toast

The last of the wedding toasts are traditionally raised by the Best Man and he has two toasts to perform: the first in response to the Groom's toast to the bridesmaids, the second to the Bride and Groom themselves.

Here are a couple of examples of wedding toasts for the Best Man:

"I'm sure the everyone would agree how beautiful the bridesmaids look and I know the bride is particularly grateful for all their help and support. So, without further ado, a toast, to the bridesmaids".

"Here's to my old friend, my new friend, my best friends. Ladies and gentlemen, please join with me in raising a toast to the Bride and Groom".

**

Brides Speech

Nowadays more Brides are keen to say a few words on their special day. It is here you can thank your guests for coming and say a special thank you to your wedding entourage. Without your family and friends, your day wouldn't have been the same.

In your wedding speech you may want to acknowledge special friends and remember loved ones who aren't there with you on the day.

151

You can dedicate part of your Bride speech to thanking your parents for their support and for everything you have been through with them so far. You can include some special moments that you have shared with them that you hold dear to your heart and will cherish forever.

In your Bride speech you will want to say a special something to your new husband; maybe a special memory that have when you first met, what was about him that made you fall in love with him and to tell him you're looking forward to the years ahead with him. Give him the recognition he deserves.

Example Brides' speech

You may well be wondering what the bride is doing making a speech. Well, those of you who know me well know that I always have talked a lot (& loudly!) and usually find a way to get my two penneth worth in so it probably is no surprise! I also wanted to say thank you to those deserving in my own words.

I feel privileged to be sharing our day with most of the friends and family who have been important to us during our lives. Many of you have travelled from afar: - America, Ireland, Switzerland, Spain and even Wales & Yorkshire to be here. Thanks to all of you for the efforts and sacrifices you have made to be with us today.

To Carol and John, thank you for making me feel so welcome in the Hearst family. Thank you for raising Steve so well, although I understand that the warranty is out of date now and the refund deadline has long since passed. I might keep him for a while though as he has so many qualities, charm, brains, and beauty are sadly the only ones missing…. and thank you also for the generous financial contribution that meant we could have a honeymoon we really wanted.

Mum - thank you for your love, support, and care over the last 29 years and for your contributions to making this such a special day.

Steve, thank you for biting the bullet, proposing and turning up today, on time and appropriately dressed. You are the love of my life, my best friend and now my husband. I don't think anybody could be happier than I am today, and I can't wait for us to share the rest of our lives together. It means a lot to be your wife & I'm sure you're happy now that you can start to let yourself go. Finally, I have some small gifts for my beautiful bridesmaids - Kath, Liz and Corinne. It's been wonderful having you all here today - I'm sure your presence has enhanced the photos no end! But seriously - thank you.

And now, I'd like you all to stand and raise your glasses in a toast to the bridesmaids…..

Bride's toast

Traditionally the bride did not make a speech, so there is no formal toast for her to make. This means she can choose to toast whoever

153

she likes. Popular choices are her parents/groom's parents and family, her bridesmaids/helpers, absent friends, particularly if one is a parent, or close relative, and/or her new husband!

Maid of Honour

Speeches are not just for the men of the wedding party. Nowadays many ladies in the entourage like to say a few words and this is a great way to say a special thank you to the couple for asking you to play an important role on their special day.

The Maid of Honour speech should be light-hearted and have just the right amount of sentiment to allow for some oohs and aaahs! The guests will love to hear some funny stories about the bride; maybe some anecdotes of when you grew up together or a special milestone that you both shared. Try to include poignant message; say something from the heart. This is a great time for you to tell the bride how much she means to you!

You can include in your Maid of Honour speech a special note about the bride's parents and maybe a happy memory if you have a relationship with them.

In the Maid of Honour speech, you should thank the other Bridesmaids for their help in making today wonderful for their friend and for being a big part of the special day. You should also compliment the ushers, finally proposing a toast.

Example speech- Maid of Honour

For those of you that don't already know me I'm Rebecca, Xanthe's 'slightly' older sister. When Xanthe first asked me to give her away, I felt two things, the first was one of extreme and enormous pride that she'd asked me, and the second was 'Oh my God' I have to do a speech. So please don't worry this won't take too long.

I would like to thank the vicar for a lovely service, the vicar's mate for keeping an eye out on the weather, although Uncle Anthony could well have had something to do with that and Victoria, Xanthe's lifelong friend and beautiful bridesmaid. I am also delighted to have my Mum, sisters and brother here today to celebrate Xanthe's (and Stuarts) day, one which I hope is the start of many more 'happiest days of their life'.

Xanthe has given me, and all of my family some incredibly happy and joyous moments over the years. She was a delight to grow up with and has always provided us with some memorable moments. Having known Xanthe all her life I have a huge library of stories to leave her embarrassed and humiliated, but out of respect for her on her big day I have decided NOT to tell them...

So, I'm not going to tell to tell you about the milkman, yes they were around in those days, asking me how my brother was on many an occasion – well done Mum, Xanthe always loved that hair cut,

And I'm not going to admit that I did my bit towards Xanthe's hairstyles when I cut her fringe to about 1cm, and it took most of the next 5 years to grow back. In fact, I'm surprised she ever forgave me! I can so clearly remember the horror on her face when I finally let her see it.

And I'm not going to mention the fact that Xanthe as a young child was at her happiest playing on her own with her fisher price toys, she liked the red headed one with the long fringe best!! – Funny that!

Xanthe, as I'm sure you all know is fiercely independent – I am reminded of a particular suitcase, small red one, that was often packed on her way to leave home for one shore or another, and this one's first outing was to go back to Yorkshire with my Uncle George, even then an old man when she was about 4 years old. As far as I can recall the only things she'd actually packed were books – and perhaps that little Fisher Price friend? When Xanthe first introduced Stuart to us all, well we weren't quite sure what to make of him really, and I'm sure Stuart felt exactly the same, I think someone coming into a family of four sisters and a brother can find the whole experience quite daunting but Stuart took it all in his stride and has since become the comedian and magician of family social events...............

ON a more serious note, I hope you all agree that the wedding so far, has been a huge success, I would like to thank all of you for celebrating the day with us especially those who have travelled almost the length of the country to be here. It has been an absolute honour for me, Xanthe, to give you away today; you are a fantastic sister, great daughter, and brilliant friend.

I've never seen you happier than you have been over these last few years with Stuart; I hope the best for you now and always

Finally, on behalf of my Mum, my sisters and brother, and of course all our partners, not forgetting Zach and Maddy, I would like to welcome Stuart, his Mum and Dad, Jill and Roy, and his brother, Pete, into our family, we all look forward to getting to know you better.

Now ladies and gentlemen, it gives me great pleasure to invite you all to stand and raise your glasses in a toast to the bride and groom, Xanthe and Stuart. To love, laughter and happily ever after – Cheers!

****

Index

****